GW00671809

THE FORGOTTEN PIONEER

A true family story set in East Africa

ANTHEA RAMSAY

Matador
9 Priory Business Park
Kibworth Beauchamp
Leicestershire LE8 0RX, UK
Tel: (+44) 116 279 2299
Fax: (+44) 116 279 2277
Email: books@troubador.co.uk
Web: www.troubador.co.uk/matador

ISBN 978 1783062 089

British Library Cataloguing in Publication Data.
A catalogue record for this book is available from the British Library.

Typeset by Troubador Publishing Ltd
Printed and bound in the UK by CPI Group (UK) Ltd

Matador is an imprint of Troubador Publishing Ltd

I have written this story about my family and their lives in Kenya as I remember it,
and do not intend to be political, controversial or to cause offence to any parties.
All photographs used in this book are either taken from our family albums,
or have been loaned to me by friends.

This book is in memory of my grandparents, George Ernest and Alice Muriel Ramsay, who were pioneers in every sense of the word. They, like so many early East African settlers, were so intent on trying to survive in this harsh, new country that they did not record their experiences, most of which are now unrecognized and lost in time. I am fortunate in having memories of my grandparents' recollections, together with letters and photographs of their early days in East Africa, without which I would not have been able to write these pages.

I have continued with stories of my parents' early lives in Africa on the fringe of the Happy Valley set and the murder of Lord Erroll, and my own childhood living in the shadow of the Mau Mau rebellion.

PROLOGUE

My grandfather first set foot in Africa in 1899, at the age of twenty-two, when it was still a primitive, undeveloped and dangerous place. He was one of the first white people with the courage and foresight to leave the comfort and security of his life in England to start a new life in a strange and distant country. In those days British East Africa was mainly uninhabited and comprised of deep, dark forests and vast plains, both of which were teeming with wild animals. What human life there was, consisted of hostile African tribes who dressed in animal skins, carried spears or poisoned arrows, used shells as their currency and had almost certainly never seen a white face.

★

RAMSAY – GEORGE ERNEST

Appointed by the Foreign Office as an Accountant to the Uganda Railway, he later resigned from the Railway to start his own accountancy business in Nairobi. He was subsequently joined by E. B. Gill, the firm being known as Ramsay and Gill, later becoming Gill and Johnson. He then became the third partner in the firm of Gailey & Roberts Ltd., and was Chairman of the company until his death in Nairobi in 1953. In 1904, he was married in Mombasa Cathedral to Alice Muriel Norman who died in Nairobi in 1950. They had two sons.

Extract concerning George Ernest Ramsay from *Tribute To The Pioneers,* by Mary Gillett, 1986.

PART ONE

CHAPTER ONE

NEW BEGINNINGS

My grandfather, George Ernest Ramsay, whom I called Grandpa, was born at 13 Sylvester Terrace, Mark House Road, Walthamstow on 11 December 1876. He was the son of George Ramsay, a fairly wealthy wine merchant, and his French wife, Clara Jeronomy (nee Le Plastrier), whose ancestors were French Huguenots who arrived in England as refugees in 1685. George Ernest was a good looking boy of medium height, large build and a mass of light brown hair which he was to lose at a very early age leaving him almost completely bald. He was one of a large family comprising nine children – two boys and seven girls, Clara, Elizabeth, Arthur, Amy, Gertrude, Winifred, Beatrice and twins Edith and my grandfather. The family lived in a comfortable, rambling old house in Bromley which they shared with their grandmother, Sophia Le Plastrier, and three servants.

Although Grandpa loved his family, he was rather self-contained and solitary by nature and often longed to escape to a quiet place, which was not easy with so many siblings. There was some respite during term-time when he was sent to boarding school at an early age, as was the custom for middle class families in England at that time. He enjoyed his school days as he excelled at all sports and was academically bright, but dreamed of one day escaping the confines of his family's strict Victorian lifestyle to seek an exciting and adventurous life in some far-flung country. On leaving school he was encouraged by his parents to train as an accountant, which he did, albeit reluctantly. It was while he was training in London that he met and fell in love with a pretty, slender, dark-haired girl from Lee in Kent, Alice Muriel Norman, my grandmother, whom I called Granny. They quickly became engaged and planned to marry as soon as possible, but fate intervened and they were destined to be apart for nearly four years.

★

Granny's parents, Charles and Alice Sophia, had four children – Alice Muriel who was born on 22 August 1876, Charles, Marguerite Annie (known as Daisy) and Katherine (known as Kitty). She was particularly close to her younger sisters who were foreordained to eventually join her in Kenya. Their brother Charles became a successful architect and was responsible for many of the buildings in Kingsway, London.

The chance for my grandfather to start a new life in Africa occurred one grey, rainy Sunday afternoon as he was sitting in the drawing room of his parents' house idly flicking through *The Times*. Suddenly his eyes focused on a large advertisement, which had been inserted by the British Government, looking for people to work in the newly opened East African Protectorate. Although he knew nothing about this part of the world, having always had a thirst for adventure, he was quick to respond to this opportunity. It was not long before he was offered a position by the Foreign Office as the accountant for The Uganda Railway where he was to be based in Nairobi, or 'Nyrobi', as it was then known. Grandpa's new job was to help curtail the spiralling costs of the building of the new railway line from Nairobi to Uganda at a salary of £200 per annum, which was a good amount to earn then. The contract stated that he was expected to learn to speak Hindustani in order to communicate with the Indian railway workers, as he would be camping and working alongside them. He was also offered a free second class passage on a steamer ship sailing to Mombasa, but decided to pay for his own ticket, choosing to leave on the first available ship and to travel first class – a wise decision, as travelling second class in those days was pretty ghastly.

The railway line had been started in Mombasa on the Kenya coast in 1896, and was planned to reach Nairobi in May 1899 when my grandfather's contract required him to start work. He was so excited to be offered this position that he did not give a second thought to the prospect of exchanging the comfort of his life in England for a tent in the middle of Africa. Neither did he consider the hardships he would have to endure, as his thoughts were concentrated on the chance of adventure and the prospect of spending many hours shooting wild animals. His friends and family, especially his fiancée, my grandmother, Alice, were shocked and confused at the speed of his decision to accept a job so far away in what was then thought of as the 'dark continent'. Although heartbroken, my grandmother promised to remain faithful to him and it was agreed that they would marry as soon as he returned to England. His contract was for two years, but no one, least of all my grandfather, imagined that he would fall under the thrall of Africa and remain there for the rest of his life.

Last photo taken of the family for my grandfather to take to Africa with him – from right back row, Edith, Clara Jeronomy, Arthur, Clara, Elizabeth and Amy. Bottom row from left, Gertrude, George and Beatrice, 1899.

CHAPTER TWO

MOMBASA

My grandfather sailed into the palm-fringed port of Mombasa, at the edge of the Indian Ocean, on board SS *Norman* in May 1899. On disembarking, he, and the other bemused passengers, were immediately surrounded by crowds of excited, gesticulating natives all fighting to row them ashore. They were unceremoniously piled onto crude, wobbly, wooden 'dug out' boats before being rowed with great exuberance to the mainland. Grandpa always said that he felt as if he had landed in Utopia at his first sight of the clear blue sea sprinkled with dhows, the thick tropical forests, herds of elephant, millions of monkeys and exotic birds. The deserted white sandy beaches, bathed in sunshine, were surrounded by plantations of tall whispering coconut palms – all so completely different from anything he had ever seen before and not at all what he expected to find in Africa. However, Mombasa was not as idyllic as it first looked as there was no piped water or sewers and it was infested with slithering puff adders, enormous rats, mosquitoes and numerous leopards roaming around the town at night.

★

Vasco da Gama, the Portuguese explorer, stumbled upon Mombasa in 1498 while travelling en route to India, although the ancient town is supposed to have been founded in about AD1000. Vasco da Gama and his crew did not stay there long as they found the Arab inhabitants threatening and hostile, but decided to continue north to the little town of Malindi where the people were much more welcoming. The discovery of ancient Chinese and Persian coins, as well as Egyptian idols, prove that many dynasties lived on the Kenya coast before the Arabs, but for hundreds of years a Swahili culture born of Arab and Swahili intermarriage had prospered here. Mombasa came under European rule in 1505 when the Portuguese captured it from the Arabs, but in 1585 the Turks came across the harbour and after a bloody battle managed to drive the Portuguese out. Approximately four years later, with the help of reinforcements from Goa, the Portuguese recaptured it and ruled the coastal strip with a barbarous hand, draining it of its many riches. Fort Jesus was built in 1591, not only to protect their trade route to India, but also their interests on the East African coast. Remarkably, the battered old walls, supposedly built in the shape of a man, remain stubbornly steadfast to this day. The Arabs and the Portuguese were constantly fighting for control of Mombasa and the fort, which finally fell into the hands of the Arabs in 1729. In 1887 the Sultan of Zanzibar granted the British East Africa Association a concession to govern these territories for a period of fifty years – he, of course, ensured that he was paid generous taxes for both the import and export trade.

On 18 April 1888, the British East Africa Association became the Imperial British East Africa Company and Mombasa was designated as the headquarters. Immediate steps were taken to improve the harbour, one of the largest natural harbours in the world, and by 1890 the long and difficult task of opening the interior from Mombasa to Uganda had begun. By the time the British Foreign Office took over the administration in 1895 it was becoming a progressive port with a rapidly developing commercial community.

Among other forms of nautical transport were the crude Arab dhows, which had been plying the Indian Ocean between Arabia and India since time immemorial bringing spices, carpets, silk, precious metals and the beautiful, ancient, ornate chests to East Africa and Zanzibar. These wonderful Arab chests were bought and treasured by many pioneers and their families – I am looking at one in our drawing room as I write.

By 1899 Mombasa was relatively civilized, with stone buildings mingling with a mixture of mud and tin huts stretching along the stinking, intricate, twisty lanes where Indian shopkeepers plied their trade. Arab men with their flowing white robes rode their fat little donkeys down the narrow lanes, often with their *bibis* (wives) covered from head to toe in black hijabs looking like eerie crows riding side saddle behind them. The pioneers travelled around in small four-wheel trolleys known locally as 'garries'. They consisted of a bench precariously balanced between an awning and a platform, which was pushed by hordes of natives at frightening speed along the old abandoned railway lines. There were many accidents in these trolleys as the makeshift handbrake often failed, resulting in the passengers being hurled dangerously to the ground. These deserted railway lines were the result of an earlier abortive attempt by the Imperial British East Africa Company to build a two-foot gauge railway line from Mombasa running sixty-five miles across the arid, scorched wilderness of the Taru Desert. The line was much too frail for the rugged African terrain and the first official journey ended in disaster with the engine being derailed, apparently after hitting a gigantic snail – there were many in Mombasa at the time. In 1890 these lines were sold off, laid along the streets of Mombasa, and subsequently used for passenger transport trolleys.

My grandfather promised himself that one day he would own a property in this idyllic place – a dream he eventually achieved. His first port of call, after a terrifying ride in a 'gari' was to report at the railway offices in Kilindini to receive further instructions. To his delight he was given a few days in Mombasa to acquire a tent, guns, a kerosene lamp and suitable clothes for his new life in the bush. He immediately purchased a tent, which he pitched under the shade of some palm trees, before excitedly proceeding to investigate this fascinating island.

★

As Grandpa was working for The Uganda Railway, he was permitted to 'hitch a ride' in a very basic open railway carriage on the partly completed steam train to the railhead at Nairobi. Other intrepid adventurers and missionaries who arrived in Kenya at the same time, or earlier, had to walk or trek by ox-wagon, often taking months to complete the hazardous journey as the train service officially started in 1903. The train crossed the bridge to the mainland over the Strait of Macupa as it slowly belched and puffed away from the steamy heat of the coast, through the thick forests and then the Taru desert, its tinderbox packed with acacia scrub fuel. It stopped frequently for several hours at various tiny makeshift stations for the boilers to be refilled with water. This gave any passengers time to disembark into the African bush to take pot shots at unsuspecting wild animals, while filling their stomachs with a strange assortment of food sold by Indian vendors from the side of the track. The train was stationary overnight and was often forced to stop during the day to allow a herd of elephant to cross the line. It is just as well that my grandfather had no idea at the time that man-eating lions were known to jump into the open-sided carriages at night and carry passengers off into the darkness.

A 'gari'

CHAPTER THREE

NAIROBI

The train eventually approached the railhead at Nairobi where the air was much cooler. As it chugged into the siding, my grandfather and the one or two other newly arrived railway officials, covered from head to toe in the thick red dust of Africa, stumbled off the train and straight into their extraordinary new lives.

★

Unlike Mombasa, Nairobi was uninhabited and undeveloped, consisting of swampy, flat land dotted with thorn trees as far as the eye could see. There were thousands of wild animals roaming the plains, as well as masses of croaking frogs. An Englishman, Ronald Preston, with a team of Indian construction workers, had just preceded them and a small camp was being established by the siding. Work soon started on laying out a rail yard for shunting, as it was necessary to break up the trains into smaller units before tackling the steep grades up the escarpment to Naivasha and on to Kisumu. The escarpment is formed by an enormous split in the earth's surface running the length of Africa which is known as the Great Rift Valley. It stretches 4,000 miles from Mozambique to Northern Syria and remains one of the most awe-inspiring sights in the world.

This inhospitable, formerly undiscovered, swampy area which had now been named 'Nairobi', was chosen as the base for the headquarters of the railway by George Whitehouse, the Chief Engineer of The Uganda Railway, mainly because the land was flat and there was a stream known as *Vaso-en-Airobe* (river of cold water) by the Maasai. Drinking water was obtained from this stream and boiled up in *debbes* (old kerosene containers). By the time the Indian railway workers had arrived here from Mombasa, where the line had been started, many had been killed by lions or died from exhaustion, dehydration and disease. Those who had survived were often ill with malaria and other life threatening illnesses and hardly able to work.

In his memoirs, Ronald Preston described Nairobi when he first saw it as: "A bleak, swampy, stretch of soppy landscape, devoid of human habitation of any sort, the resort of thousands of wild animals of every species. It did not boast a single tree".

Nairobi was an extremely miserable place to be based as there were no sanitary arrangements of any kind and illnesses such as typhoid, malaria and black water fever were rife. Only the luckiest and most resilient pioneer survived, as anyone unfortunate enough to become ill had no doctors or hospitals to help them. They also had to contend with poisonous snakes, dangerous animals and threatening, suspicious African tribes who had wandered into the area with poisoned arrows. I often wonder whether Grandpa really knew what he was letting himself in for when he so eagerly accepted the job with The Uganda Railway.

My grandfather pitched his tent close to the one or two other white officials, with the many Indian railway workers camped nearby. The pioneers shared their evening meal of zebra, bushbuck, ostrich or wart hog in front of the fire on which the meat had earlier been cooked. After the African sun slipped over the edge of the earth and darkness fell, suddenly and silently, they retired to their tents with their guns and a kerosene lamp for comfort and safety. It was dangerous to venture out after darkness had fallen, as apart from the obvious threats the whole area consisted of a series of game pits. These deep pits were used by the natives who lay in wait with their poisoned arrows for animals to come and drink from the nearby stream. Many people have since questioned George Whitehouse's decision to choose this particular unsuitable spot as a base for the railway.

Nairobi, 1899

Nairobi, 1900

As he lay alone in his fragile tent, Grandpa, although he never admitted it, must have felt very vulnerable as he listened to the roar of hundreds of lions coming from every direction as they rampaged around the camp. Fires were lit and tent flaps kept tightly closed, not only to keep the nocturnal animals at bay, but also against the unfriendly, forbidding darkness and the ever-present threat of bandits. Despite the dangers, I'm sure he enjoyed the novelty of listening to the night orchestra of insects and animals, vying against the many croaking frogs as he fell asleep under the starry African skies.

My grandfather's tent

The tents the railway workers and officials lived in were very basic and extremely uncomfortable. During the rainy season the ground sheets sank into the stinking, muddy bog of black cotton, but a few months later the ground became as hard as rock, before cracking up and choking the occupants in thick red dust. Their bedding was an invitation for every kind of snake or insect to burrow into, including deadly scorpions.

★

The British Government sent George Whitehouse to Kenya sometime before 1896 to supervise the building of the railway line from Mombasa to Uganda. This huge project took over five years to complete with the track eventually crossing through forests, plains, swamps and escarpments. It also ran through the grazing land of the Maasai and the Kikuyu homelands. The Maasai mainly accepted this invasion in fairly good spirits, but the Kikuyu were not so happy and remained hostile for many years. The natives were amazed at the whole project, as they had never seen anything like it and for years referred to the railway line as the 'iron snake'. However the building of this virtually single-track line turned out to be a hugely impractical and challenging assignment, undertaken in appalling conditions and costing the British Government far more than they had ever bargained for. It was even dubbed 'The Lunatic Line' by the British press after it became known how much it was costing the taxpayer.

About thirty-two thousand workers, mainly Sikhs, were shipped from India to build the line, many of whom lost their lives or had to be repatriated through ill heath and replaced. There were numerous other problems including the bad behavior of some of the Indian manual workers who started using the young and innocent native women as prostitutes, which further antagonized the already hostile natives. On one occasion this led to an uprising at Kedong when the Maasai attacked the railway workers, killing about 500 of them, after two Maasai girls had been raped. This led to a counter attack by an English railway worker, Andrew Dick, who unfortunately ran out of ammunition and was speared to death by the Maasai. These problems were eventually solved, by bringing the workers' wives and children from India to join their husbands, many of whom remained in East Africa and subsequently became successful men and women owning important businesses.

★

My grandfather on the bridge while building the railway line, 1900

Building the railway line, 1900

Winston Churchill, who visited Kenya as Under Secretary of State for the Colonies in 1907, said of the railway:

> The British art of 'muddling through' was here seen in one of its finest expositions. Through everything – through forests, through ravines, through troops of marauding lions, through famine, through war, through five years of excoriating Parliamentary debate, muddled and marched the railway.

Pioneers talked a lot about lions, as I have done in this memoir, as to them they were the most detested and feared of animals – there were so many of them that they were thought of as vermin by the pioneers. Grandpa had never had any reason to use a gun in England, consequently, when he first arrived in Kenya he was a pretty awful shot. He found it fairly simple to take pot shots at various bushbuck, zebra, ostrich, and giraffe, but lions were a different matter. They were not so easy to kill and if wounded, as they often were, turned on their aggressor. Lions were the cause of many problems, but most worryingly while building the bridge across the Tsavo River in 1898 they acquired a taste for eating people, with many Indian railway workers being killed in this way. In 1900 an Irish railway official, Joseph O'Hara, who was working and living with his wife and children in Voi, near Nairobi, was dragged from his tent while sleeping. His petrified wife woke to find the lion standing two feet away from her eating her husband.

Grandpa loved telling me a gruesome story about an incident that occurred when he first arrived in Nairobi and was returning from Mombasa after a business trip – for some reason I loved this story and persuaded him to repeat it time and time again. On 6 June 1900, he was travelling in an adjoining carriage to that of his friend, the Assistant Superintendent of Railway Police, Charles Henry Ryall, and two colleagues, a German, Paul Huebner and an Italian, Arnaldo Parenti, who were travelling from Mombasa in Ryall's inspection carriage, which had been joined to the train, to suppress a strike caused by some Indian railway workers. Aware that the train stopped overnight at Kimaa (Swahili for minced meat) about 255 miles from Mombasa, which was rife with man-eating lions, they arranged to take it in turns for one of them to keep watch. When it was Charles Ryall's turn to stay awake, he must have dozed off as my grandfather was woken to the sound of blood-curdling screams. He was forced to watch in horror as a lion jumped out of the carriage with his friend, Charles Ryall, in his mouth and proceeded to devour him at the side of the track. I now know that this episode is well documented, in varying versions, but not quite as my grandfather told it!

Kikuyu Viaducts, 1900

Camping at Fort Ternan near Kisumu, 1901

In letters written to his sisters from his tent, Grandpa mentions how uncomfortable, lonely and bored he was when he first arrived in Kenya as there were not many other pioneers to befriend at that stage, and certainly not many based at the railway camp in Nairobi. All his spare time was spent shooting animals, not just for the excitement or to eat, but because there was nothing else to do. In one of his letters, written from his tent to his sister, Clara, on 18 February 1900, he thanks her for the Christmas pudding she had lovingly sent by steamer ship from England and after talking about family matters, he continues:

Last Sunday I borrowed a nag and rode with another fellow to a farm where there is an English family living, they have not long come from the Straits Settlements where they had a plantation. There is one son who owns the farm, and his mother and four sisters. They seem very nice people and have invited us to come up there as often as we like. The girls remind me of the Carr girls, as they are very angular and are possessed of an overly strong jaw. The brother, I like very much, he is coming to my place to scoff next Sunday. He seems to have made friends with the natives already, but at a price, as when he first arrived here, which was some months before the others, he was shot with a poisoned arrow, but he managed to get over it, which greatly surprised the natives, as they think it is impossible to live after having being shot by one, so now they imagine him as some sort of God and the Chiefs are always making him presents of gourds and bows and arrows, it seems as if they would do anything for him so as to win favour in his eyes.

I am afraid that it would be impossible to keep a diary of my doings, as you suggest, as it is precisely the same thing every day without any variation. You see I am at work from 10 till 4 as it gets dark at 6.30. There is very little chance of shooting as the D.O. has issued an order that you are to go 3 miles out from the station to shoot in case of stray shots. Of course at Railhead I had plenty of time to shoot in the day. I intend getting a weeks leave and going for a long shoot as soon as I get an opportunity. I had my photo taken outside my tent, but the chap who took it has gone up to the lake, but I daresay I will be able to get a copy when he comes back, and will send you one. Have not yet got that box you sent me with the pudding, but as soon as I get a chance I shall run down to the coast and see if I can come across it. I hope Eddie will get some skating, it's a long time since there was any at home. I wish I could write a longer letter, but really can't think of anything more, so give my love to Mother and Dad and everybody at home. Believe me to be your affectionate brother, George.

Grandpa seemed delighted by the invitation from his new friend to visit his farm, which probably consisted of land with a couple of tents, and the prospect of some female company, despite the fact that his friend's sisters had what he describes as an 'overly strong jaw' – I never discovered the name of the family with these unfortunate daughters! He was obviously extremely envious that his new comrade had become friendly with the natives so quickly, which shows how sensitive this issue was.

Gradually more pioneers began to arrive in Nairobi and the need for food other than fresh meat became a huge problem. Some enterprising Indian railway workers, who had completed their contracts with The Uganda Railway, started selling items imported from India, such as canned butter (which was usually rancid) from tin shacks which had been erected near the railway camp. Nairobi also now had a doctor, Dr Rosendo Ayres Ribeiro, a young pioneer from Goa, who lived in a tent, practiced from a tin shed and visited his patients while riding a tame zebra. In 1902 he diagnosed an outbreak of bubonic plague when everything, including the hastily built timber and iron railway station and all the Indian shacks had to be burnt down. It was not long before a new shanty town of tin huts – Nairobi was often referred to as 'Tinsville' then – sprung up around the railway siding. It continued to grow in a haphazard way into what is now the thriving capital of Kenya. Unfortunately the many slums in Nairobi still resemble the 'Tinsville' of 1900.

When he wasn't working, or sometimes as part of his job, Grandpa loved to trek for miles on shooting expeditions with his gun bearer, either pitching his tent in the middle of the bush or stopping at remote camps such as Fort Ternan, 50 km from Kisumu. Armed with elephant guns they proceeded by foot through forests and plains, enjoying the tremendous sense of freedom and space. He once shot an enormous buffalo of which he was immensely proud. Its head adorned a wall in every house our family subsequently lived in until my mother, who hated it, eventually arranged for it to be buried in the garden of our home in Muthaiga. Although there were many dangerous animals roaming the plains, buffalo were the most respected as they were liable to charge without provocation and could move deceptively fast. Grandpa also loved to fish in what is now Lake Naivasha, but was then known as *Nai Posha* by the Maasai, meaning 'rough water' due to the sudden storms that often occurred around the lake in the afternoon, whipping the serenity of the calm mornings into a frenzy of lashing rain.

Lion shot by my grandfather, Nairobi, 1900

My grandfather shooting next to the railhead, 1900

The killing of a zebra, Nairobi, 1905

Travelling by ox-wagon on a hunting trip, 1905

CHAPTER FOUR

LIFE-LONG FRIENDSHIPS

I t was crucial for the early pioneers to form friendly relationships with the natives, who in most cases resented these strange white interlopers who did not speak their language, had strange ways, and were camping on their land. My grandfather was determined to overcome this problem, soon learning their languages and establishing relationships of mutual respect and trust which lasted throughout his life. There were many different African tribes of whom the nomadic Maasai, the formidable Nandi and the suspicious, unfriendly Kikuyu were dominant. The Maasai were, and still are, arguably the most interesting and colourful of all the tribes. They are tall, proud warriors many of whom carry spears to this day, paint their faces, wear vibrant loincloths and adorn themselves with beaded necklaces and bracelets. According to Maasai lore they originally migrated from north of Lake Turkana, reaching the Ngong Hills in the seventeenth century, but by the time the early pioneers arrived their land stretched over many areas.

One of the most curious customs practiced by the Maasai is to extract the two front teeth from their lower jaw, while another trait is that of distorting the lobe of the ear by stretching it until it hangs down about five inches. They then pierce the lobes and stick pieces of carved wood or little tin canisters hanging from a chain through the hole, but these days they are more likely to embellish their ear lobes with brightly coloured beads. When my grandfather first arrived in Kenya, the Maasai men wore tall furry headdresses made from monkey skin, animal skin loincloths and little bells on their ankles to announce their approach. The young pioneers were terrified of the Maasai warriors, *Elmorani*, who, when on the war-path wore ferocious looking headdresses made of black ostrich feathers and carried a shield with a spear suspended from a raw-hide waist belt.

Traditionally the Maasai's only possessions are their highly valued, humpbacked, scrawny cattle from which they take the 'blood of life' sucking it from a hole made by shooting an arrow into the neck of the cow before plugging the wound with a wad of dung and mud. They drink the milk, which they sometimes mix with blood and honey, before storing it in brightly decorated gourds. They believe that this diet will make them strong, which is particularly important for the young men who were once expected to kill a lion with one stroke of a spear to prove their Manhood. At night, their precious cattle are herded into a compound surrounded by thorn bushes to protect them from wild animals, while the Maasai crawl into their beehive shaped huts which are erected using branches, twigs, cow dung and urine. These huts are not high enough for the tall Maasai to stand up in, therefore, they crawl through a small opening and sit or sleep curled up on beds made of branches with animal skins to keep them warm during the cold nights. They usually live in groups of between eight to fifteen families and when they move on to their next destination, herding their cattle over the vast empty plains, everything is burnt to the ground as if no one had ever lived there. Today, many Maasai have become more sophisticated and moved into the towns, while some of them still live by their old traditions on what little land is left for them. Most early pioneers learned to speak the Maa dialect, and some began to idolize the Maasai as they were fascinated by their traditions and fearlessness which naturally appealed to these tough rather gung-ho young men. A few eventually went as far as to live and associate only with the Maasai, spurning their fellow countrymen.

★

My grandfather soon began to form friendships with other pioneers, some of whom had preceded him, namely Ewart Scott Grogan, Major James Hamilton Gailey and David Oliver Roberts (known as Robbie). He formed a particularly strong bond with David Roberts and James Gailey who had shared the hell of the early days in Nairobi with him. They were surveyors, who like Grandpa, had come to Kenya from the United Kingdom to work for The Uganda Railway. James Gailey had arrived in 1896 and David Roberts in 1897. Most of these tough, indomitable pioneers were from privileged backgrounds, but had no money, only the foresight and vision to see what the future of this colony held.

There was not much in the way of entertainment or social life for them, and what little there was revolved mainly around the bi-annual race meetings with African jockeys riding Somali ponies. Pioneers trekked to Nairobi by ox-wagon from their remote farms, often travelling for miles through the bush with their tents for these special occasions. In 1901, my grandfather, together with one or two other railway officials, helped to found the original Nairobi Railway Club, which was situated in a large corrugated-iron shed. The club provided another much needed social meeting place where politics were discussed and many a business deal signed. Being an enthusiastic cricket player, he ensured that a cricket pitch was eventually prepared near the club where he and his cronies could indulge in their favourite game. It is recorded that: "George Ernest Ramsay attended the first meeting of the Committee of Europeans in Nairobi on 4th February 1902".

Major James Hamilton Gailey

David Oliver Roberts

In the same year, Sir Charles Norton Eliot, the governor of the East Africa Protectorate and progenitor of the colonial settlement, established The Crown Lands ordinance scheme backed by the Foreign Office, which was dedicated to recruiting people from the Empire to farm this fertile and so far wasted land. This project was mainly designed to make The Uganda Railway, which was by then in huge financial trouble, pay for itself partly by handling freight such as farm machinery from the coast to the 'highlands' where the new settlers were establishing their farms. The plan attracted many new pioneers and by 1904 people were arriving from all over the world, all hoping to start a new and prosperous life in British East Africa. Many were British aristocrats who were not going to inherit the family title or had been banished in disgrace, while others were intrepid adventurers bored with life at home. Most wanted to farm the green and productive land and were prepared to work hard and take risks, but many were just wasters and speculators.

Kikuyu, 1903

Maasai, 1903

Under this British Government scheme a million acres of land was being disposed of at three to four pounds an acre, and for those with courage and endurance the rewards were high. The land was being sold on 999-year leases and the contract required a capital sum to be invested in the first five years with an annual rent paid to the government. There was, of course, a mad scramble to take advantage of this amazing offer. People pitched tents outside the Lands Office where they often remained for months while they waited for their land applications to be approved. During this time there were many fights and disagreements among the frustrated settlers as they waited in hope, while inexperienced civil servants totally mismanaged the whole project. The scheme did not endear the white population to the Africans as their land was supposed to be protected by law. However, this was overlooked in the rush and much of the nomadic grazing land belonging to the Maasai in the Rift Valley, as well as land belonging to the Kikuyu, was allotted to the white settlers.

★

On 7 July 1902, Grandpa left The Uganda Railway as his contract had ended. Although he desperately missed my grandmother, he decided that he did not want to return to England as planned but to stay in Kenya. Granny, who also had an adventurous streak, was thrilled at the thought of making a new life in Africa and was eager to join him as soon as she could, but it was not possible at that stage as he had no job and still lived in a tent.

Grandpa had always loved Mombasa and decided that this was where he was going to live and work. He was soon offered a position, with a good salary, as an accountant working for Anderson and Myers' Trading and Development Company. Impatient for my grandmother to join him, after arranging for her to sail to Mombasa on the next available ship, he purchased a small piece of land on the deserted beach in Port Reitz, part of Mombasa's inner harbour. Here, he proudly built a small mud and wattle shack where he intended to bring his bride and start their married life. However, this was not to be, as being astute, ambitious and an entrepreneur, he was quick to see the benefits of the Crown Lands ordinance scheme and decided to return to Nairobi to join the quest for land. On 23 August 1904 he was allotted his first stretch of land in Dagoretti Road.

CHAPTER FIVE

ALICE

My grandmother, Alice, sailed into the port of Mombasa on the SS *Juba* just as my grandfather had done more than four years earlier, with a feeling of trepidation and excitement as she was reunited with her future husband. Although Granny was only 5'2" and slight, she was stoical, strong-willed and courageous. She must also have been very much in love with my grandfather to have waited so patiently before joining him in Africa.

Single women were not usually permitted entry into Kenya unless they were missionaries or engaged to someone who was already living there, in which case they normally married immediately on arrival. George Ernest Ramsay and Alice Muriel Norman, accordingly, took their marriage vows in the partly completed Mombasa Cathedral on 2 June 1904, a few days after her arrival. Granny wore a pretty starched white cotton dress with a lace frill round a low neckline, a corsage of fresh flowers pinned to her chest and white embroidered slippers on her feet, all chosen appropriately for a marriage in the heat of the tropics. Their honeymoon was spent in the rather optimistically named Grand Hotel, a run-down and somewhat primitive place. It had the usual *makuti* roof, dark, deep verandas, was surrounded by tall coconut palms and overlooked the sea. They then travelled in what I consider to be the most romantic, if not the most comfortable train in the world, to their new home in Nairobi. Although the train had only officially been operating for a year, the three first class carriages were very smart with mahogany panelling and padded green leather seating. There was a separate room with a basin and lavatory, and a large private area in the front of the carriage where the luggage was stored. The open windows were covered with wire netting, which successfully kept the mosquitoes out, but also let huge clouds of thick red dust in. The second class carriages were very different and consisted of large open-sided carriages with wooden benches on either side.

My grandmother's excited anticipation increased as the steam train chugged away from the intense, steamy heat of Mombasa and into the hills, through plantations of coconut and baobab trees, weaving westward through the starlit night onwards to Nairobi. The train stopped at every station, including the tropical station of Mazeras and the aptly named Simba (Swahili for lion) station where man-eating lions had so recently roamed. A welcome cup of tea was taken in a Dak bungalow at one of the little stations before continuing to Voi, some ninety miles uphill from Mombasa. The passengers disembarked here for dinner in another similar bungalow, which was really a corrugated-iron shack situated at the side of the tracks, where they were served a typical meal of thin 'Windsor' soup, tough boiled gazelle meat, tinned peaches and custard. Brandy and cigars were taken outside, while the passengers waited for the bell informing them the train was ready to leave.

My grandmother, Alice, on her wedding day, Mombasa, 1904

They returned from dinner to find the carriages glowing welcomingly from the kerosene lamps in each compartment, their seating area now transformed into comfortable bunks with crisp white sheets and blankets. I doubt they slept very well, as the carriages were renowned for jolting so violently as the train gained speed at night that anyone wearing false teeth was likely to find them on the floor of the compartment in the morning!

My grandfather boarding the train at Nairobi station, 1908

The vista changed while the passengers slept. On waking, my grandmother peeped though the window of the train where she had her first sight of herds of every species of wild animal, grazing on scrubland, as far as the eye could see – Africa – just as she had dreamed it would be like. The passengers then disembarked again for a breakfast of eggs, bacon, toast and tea at Makindu, before the train resumed its pace towards Athi River. As it approached Nairobi, some three hundred miles from Mombasa, the air was fresher and enticing glimpses of a snowcapped Mount Kilimanjaro, the highest mountain in Africa, could be seen from time to time. On finally completing their journey, the passengers arrived at Nairobi station to be met by hordes of excited, near-naked natives who still flocked in awe to see the miracle of the weekly arrival of the train. This shocked Granny who had never seen a black person, let alone one wearing hardly any clothes!

My grandfather sat proudly, with my grandmother beside him, as they trekked through the rough game tracks, the convoy of ox-wagons piled high with her treasured possessions, wobbling precariously, as they made their way to her first home in Nairobi. This could only be described as a two-room shack, which was constructed of wooden planks with an unlined tin roof and an earth and wattle floor, in an area later known as Kiburu road on Railway Hill. The 'long-drop' was situated in a separate mud hut, and consisted of an eight-foot pit fitted with a wooden box hanging over the hole in the ground. The zinc tub for bathing was placed at the side of the house between two sheets of corrugated iron. Rainwater for cooking and bathing was collected in debbes, which worked out well in the rainy season, but became a bit of a problem in the dry season. The kitchen also consisted of two sheets of corrugated iron, angled together like the bathroom. Part of another old debbe was placed over the remnants of a fire, which was used for cooking and heating water. Not surprisingly, Granny found life in Africa rather strange and daunting after the comforts of England, and it is difficult to imagine how she must have felt on seeing her new home for the first time.

Their humble dwelling was furnished with an assortment of antique furniture and silver from her family home in Kent, interspersed with upturned packing cases, which served as makeshift tables, standing on the mud and wattle floor. Their bed was a wooden stretcher covered with Colobus monkey skins to protect them against the chill of the African nights. The furniture, including the legs of the bed, were placed in tins of paraffin to keep away the rats and the soldier ants, known as *siafu* in Swahili, which given half a chance marched purposefully through and over everything. These ants are treated with great fear and respect, as once on their determined pursuit they are capable of devouring everything in their sights, including live flesh.

My grandparents loved their first simple abode, never tiring of being spectators to the spellbinding, never-ending theatre of wild animals viewed against the backdrop of the vast African scrubland. There were a few other wood and iron shacks, mud huts and tents inhabited by fellow pioneers scattered around in the distance, interspersed with rough animal tracks. These tracks became dusty and cracked in the dry season and flooded by swampy red mud in the rainy season. They were also used by wagons pulled by six to eight oxen, and herded by a crowd of happily chattering natives cracking *kibokos* (whips made of rhino hide). Apart from riding zebras or donkeys, ox-wagons were the only mode of transport available in Kenya.

Evenings were spent with their room romantically lit by kerosene lamps, listening to the growl and roar of the lions, very often too close for comfort, in harmony with the croaking of the frogs and chirp of the crickets. Lions in those early days had a habit of sitting right outside the house in a row and just roaring, which must have been terrifying for my grandmother when she first arrived. I suppose they were attracted by the lamps and curious at hearing human voices.

The evening meal consisted of freshly shot game cooked over an open fire by their African servant, Owino, who was to stay loyally with our family for many years.

Killing a Lion, Nairobi

Friends moving house, literally!

Owino wore nothing but a soft leather *shirka* but Granny soon, diplomatically, persuaded him to wear a long white *kanzu* with a red fez which she felt was much more appropriate. As her Swahili improved, she hesitatingly started to teach him some English recipes, which were cooked to perfection in a *sufaria* (an iron pot) over the open fire in the same primitive way as the game was cooked. Fresh meat was, of course, always plentiful and was kept in a wire safe with its legs in the obligatory tins of paraffin – no vegetarian would have existed for long in Africa then!

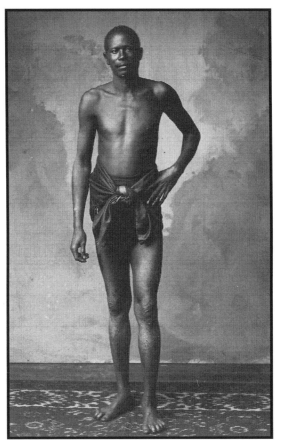

Owino, 1904

In an attempt to keep up certain standards their meals were served 'in style' using my grandmother's fine bone china and Georgian silver, as they ate off their upturned packing case which served as a makeshift dining room table. Before retiring to bed, Owino filled their zinc bathtub with hot water, which had been heated up in debbes over the same open fire over which their meal had been prepared earlier. Visiting the 'long-drop' during the night was quite a performance, as it was essential to remember to take a kerosene lamp and a rifle with them. On numerous occasions Granny encountered poisonous snakes curled up on, or near, the seat and other nocturnal animals lurking in the bushes nearby. She once returned to find a leopard about to spring onto her bed, which caused considerable alarm at the time, but much later became an amusing anecdote to repeat at the dinner table.

Shopping for provisions was the highlight of Granny's week. She sat upright in the ox-cart with her trusted servant, Owino, next to her as they travelled down the only cleared cart track in Nairobi. This track was proudly labelled 'Government Road' and was flanked on both sides by makeshift, open-fronted Indian *dukas* (shops), which were erected out of old tin paraffin barrels. The supplies available at the time were very limited, but there was always a wonderful intoxicating array of spices and herbs, which had been transported to the port of Mombasa on the Arab dhows from Zanzibar and the Middle East.

It was de rigueur for the ladies in Kenya to wear long khaki or beige skirts made of calico, often lined with red silk as it was thought that the colour red gave added protection from the harsh equatorial sun. A starched white blouse, thick socks, laced boots and a hard topi, made from the pith of an Indian swamp plant, completed the ensemble. These hard hats, which were imported from India, were not only worn by men, women and children whenever they ventured into the sun but also indoors, as the perception at the time was that the sun could penetrate through the tin roofs of the buildings. The pioneers were extremely wary of the sun and every possible attempt was made to protect their bodies from it, as they believed that not only could it affect the spine, heart, spleen and nervous system, but also their brains! Many people even went as far as to wear spine pads made of thick wads of quilted cotton, which were attached to the back of their necks down to their buttocks. They must have been extremely uncomfortable and hot.

★

Researchers, writers and historians invariably bestow upon the pioneers the qualities of fearlessness, endurance and vision, which they undoubtedly possessed, but there is no denying that at the same time most of them were extremely eccentric. They probably would not have survived had they not been.

CHAPTER SIX

RAGS TO RICHES

My grandfather had originally gone to Kenya to seek adventure and not riches, but during the next few years, with the support of my equally enterprising and intrepid grandmother, he began buying as much land as he could on the outskirts, and in central Nairobi. Using local Indian craftsmen and materials imported from India, he began constructing many of the buildings in the town which he rented out to businessmen as shops or offices. One of the buildings was bought by Whiteaway, Laidlaw and became one of the largest stores in Nairobi, and in about 1908 Grandpa was responsible for building the main Nairobi post office in Sixth Avenue (now Kenyatta Avenue) after the original wood and iron post office had burned down in 1906. If a blue flag was flying from the post office it meant that the ship carrying mail from England had docked at Aden, while a white flag showed that the ship had safely reached Mombasa, and a red flag denoted that the mail had been sorted and was ready for distribution. It was then dispatched by armed runners, who delivered it, not only locally, but also to outlying farms. This was a dangerous job with many of the postal workers being killed by animals or bandits while carrying out this task.

Over the years Grandpa continued his pursuit for land. He bought large stretches in more remote areas, such as plantations of palm trees in Mombasa near his small mud and wattle house on the beach at Port Reitz. He also invested in many acres of fertile land in Nakuru and much later bought a six hundred-acre coffee farm, which he purchased from Lady Delamere. The farm was originally called 'Kasarini', but after he bought it he renamed it 'Kiltannon'. It was situated in Kiambu, a beautiful undeveloped area not far from Nairobi. Lady Delamere had purchased this land as an investment in 1904 and employed a manager, Leonard Wood, to establish and then manage a coffee farm. She ensconced him in a smart prefab house, which had been imported in sections at great expense from England. It had woodblock floors, a long veranda and ceilings decorated with a floral pattern in pressed steel. It was certainly one of the smartest houses in Kenya at that time. Leonard Wood was the second farmer to successfully grow coffee in Kiambu, which was quite a feat as apart from coping with constant droughts, plant disease and locusts, Kiambu was still teeming with wild animals. He and his farm labourers cleared the land of dense high bush and trees by hand before planting out the tender coffee seedlings. After all this hard work it was not known whether coffee would flourish in the area or not, but luckily the ground and climate were perfect and the farm eventually became very successful.

Many new farmers bravely took the risk of planting coffee, tea, sisal and pyrethrum. They were often undercapitalized, and not only ignorant about the land and crops they strove to grow, but also about the customs, tribal distinctions and beliefs of the people they employed. As most African tribes are pastoral it was impossible to know which crops would grow successfully in the different areas, and the farmers were usually as inexperienced as their farm workers. Many settlers had trekked to the 'highlands', or 'up country' as they referred to anywhere more than fifty miles from Nairobi. Having arrived at their destination, they set up camp in tents or mud huts whilst slowly building their timber and wattle houses, as they attempted to grow their chosen crop, starting the process of trial and error, which would test the most intrepid pioneer.

Nairobi c. 1912

Nairobi c. 1912

Nairobi post office, my grandfather built the front part before it was extended

On a picnic c. 1912

Friends trekking from Ruiru to Nairobi to visit my grandparents, 1912

Friends travelling on a 'gari', 1913

My grandmother had not been in Kenya for long before she was, not surprisingly, expecting her first child. She was understandably rather nervous at the thought of giving birth in a country where there were no proper medical facilities or hospitals, and where many babies died. In those days if anyone was unfortunate enough to require an operation it was usually performed on the dining room table, by an inexperienced doctor and without an anesthetic – just a very large tot of brandy. Needless to say the patient often died. Consequently, it was decided that Granny should return to Lee in Kent to spend the first few months of the baby's life with her family. She was especially excited at the prospect of seeing her sisters again, eager to regale them with the stories of her adventurous life in Africa and hoping to persuade them to join her there one day. Heavily pregnant, she sailed to England on a steamer ship on 27 February 1905, and George Norman entered this world on 15 May 1905. However, it was eighteen months before my grandfather saw his son for the first time, when he travelled to England to visit his family and escort his wife and child home. Although very happy to see his parents, sisters and brother again he did not dally in Kent for long, as he was not interested in spending any more time than was necessary in England. He was always impatient with the social niceties expected at that time and eager to return to his beloved Africa. He only returned to England once more during his life.

Friends establishing a farm in Ruiru

In the period my grandmother had been away many changes had occurred in Nairobi, which in 1907 had become the capital of British East Africa after the government relocated there from Mombasa. The pioneers had done much to change Nairobi into a thriving little town, which now boasted the newly completed Norfolk Hotel, freshly planted gum trees and more cleared cart tracks with proper street names. Now that my grandparents had a child, they moved into a little timber house on stilts with a green corrugated-roof which they had built on two acres close to their first dwelling on Railway Hill. It consisted of two bedrooms, a sitting room, kitchen and a veranda running the length of the house. This was the house my maternal grandmother, known as Gagee, lived in many years later. My grandparents loved their first real home, and it was here that Granny began making friends with some of the other wives who were starting to join their pioneer husbands in Kenya.

The main room in my grandparents' house in Parklands

In 1909 they moved house again, this time to Parklands, another undeveloped area just outside Nairobi, where they built their first brick house in what is now known as 3rd Avenue. Much to my grandmother's annoyance many species of wild animals, particularly wart hogs, constantly wandered into the garden trampling over everything and destroying her precious flowers and plants.

At about the same time Grandpa started his own accountancy firm in Nairobi. As there were not many accountants in Kenya, he suggested that his friend, Ernest Beasley Gill, who lived in England, might like to join him in this venture. Ernest was thrilled to be offered this wonderful opportunity and sailed to Kenya on the next available ship. This was a very successful move for both of them as the business thrived and Ernest eventually became a partner. The company was named Ramsay & Gill. In 1915 my grandfather decided that he wanted to pursue other interests and sold his partnership to a local accountant, Percy Johnson, when it became Gill and Johnson. This small company started by my grandfather all those years ago has now been taken over by Deloitte with branches both in Nairobi and Mombasa, and at the time of writing has eleven partners and approximately three hundred staff.

★

Just after the First World War Grandpa acquired a share in Gailey and Roberts, a business in which he had great confidence. Known locally as 'G & R', the company was founded in 1904 by his two friends, Major James Gailey and David Oliver Roberts. They started it as a hardware store, surveyor and estate agency business, but it later became the cornerstone for the settler farmer community by supplying agricultural equipment to outlying farms. Gailey & Roberts indirectly helped to improve the ailing profits of The Uganda Railway, as the equipment was imported from England and then transported by train from Mombasa to their showrooms in Nairobi, before being sent by rail to the 'highlands'. However, David Roberts died on 2 April 1915 of black water fever and not long thereafter James Gailey married his widow, Gladys, with whom he had been having an affair for some years. In 1924 my grandfather became the third partner with James Gailey and his wife Gladys, when Gailey & Roberts became a limited company. It was decided not to change the name to 'Gailey and Ramsay' as it was so well known by the original name. They soon began diversifying by selling cars and household goods as well as the agricultural equipment which was responsible for the company's success in the past. By 1925 Gailey & Roberts boasted five branches, in addition to having been appointed the Caterpillar tractor dealer for East Africa. My grandfather eventually became Managing Director and Chairman of this company, a title he held until his death.

★

Winston Churchill also observed after his visit to Kenya in 1907: "Everywhere hard work, strained resources, hopes persisting through many disappointments, stout hospitable hearts and the beginning, at any rate, of progress". He also warned: "There are already in miniature all the elements of keen racial and political discord".

★

The settlers now travelled everywhere by rickshaw, which had replaced the ox-wagon, and households vied with each other in their attempt to dress their rickshaw men in smarter livery than their neighbour. To complement this new fashion, the 'wild west' type of attire worn by the ladies in Kenya when my grandparents first arrived was now replaced by long, pretty, starched cotton dresses or skirts often decorated with lace. Despite this ultra-feminine look, women still carried guns strapped discreetly to their waists, wore laced up boots and a topi to keep the sun off their heads, while large elaborate hats were worn on smart occasions.

The Norfolk Hotel had become the favourite stomping ground for the pioneers to discuss hunting, business deals, farming issues and, of course, to let off steam round the bar. Everybody knew each other, and in the early days land was often sold and business deals signed informally over a few drinks. There is a story that Lord Delamare and his friends were becoming extremely boisterous one evening, when the manager, politely, asked them all to leave as it was closing time. Lord Delamere was in no mood to end the fun and locked the poor man in the meat safe along with some animal carcasses, leaving him there until the early hours when the party eventually broke up. Vociferous guests often ended up throwing furniture, or each other, out of the windows of the hotel, and during race week, riding their horses into the dining room and jumping them over the tables and chairs.

★

George Norman now attended the only school in Kenya, a Dame school, owned and run by Miss Secombe and staffed mainly by spinsters. It was co-

45

educational and accepted day and full-time boarding pupils. George started at the school as a boarder when he was only five-years old and remained there until he was fifteen, when he continued his education at Dover College in England. My grandparents would have preferred him to have attended a boarding school in England much earlier, but this was not possible due to the difficulty of travelling during and just after the First World War.

It didn't take much persuasion to tempt Granny's younger sister, Daisy, to leave England and settle in Kenya, starting her new life living with my grandparents in their home in Parklands. Being attractive and popular, especially with the many bachelors in Nairobi, she had a wonderful time being wined and dined, travelling through the makeshift roads by rickshaw, dodging potholes and wild animals, with only the moon to show them the way. Daisy was engaged four times before finally, at the age of forty, meeting and marrying a charming Irish man, Charles Riley. My grandmother was relieved that her wayward younger sister was safely 'off her hands', but sorry that they lived so far away in Kampala where Charles managed a cotton ginning business. In 1919 Daisy gave birth to a daughter, Joan Pamela (known as Pam), and they continued to enjoy life in Kampala until Charles died of diabetes when Pam was only seven years old.

Daisy brought her daughter back to live in Nairobi, where my grandparents looked after them financially, giving them a pretty little timber house with a lattice veranda in Genward Road. My grandmother took Pam 'under her wing' and generously paid for her education, which was completed in England. Soon after Daisy's arrival, Kitty, decided to join her sisters in Kenya.

Kitty instantly embraced the African lifestyle, often travelling around Nairobi on a tame Zebra. However, it was not long before she fell in love with Henry Thompson and left Kenya to settle in Scotland, where they produced three children, Drummond, Jean and William. After leaving Kenya, Kitty, who was very enterprising, established a business making various types of home-made pies and this company eventually became a thriving and very successful countrywide operation named Tickey Snacks.

My grandmother's sister, Daisy Norman's marriage to Charles Riley (my grandparents, 2nd on right, Kitty with Henry Thomson on left), Muthaiga, 1917

Kitty, my grandmother's sister, 1917

CHAPTER SEVEN

A BABY BORN IN AFRICA

My father, Derek, was the first baby in our family to be born in Kenya, on 7 September 1912 at the partly completed Nairobi Hospital. My grandmother was bitterly disappointed that she had produced another boy and not the longed-for girl. Consequently, for the first few years of his life he was dressed in pretty dresses and bonnets, with his hair left to grow into long golden curls. We have photographs of him as a baby lying in a hammock balanced between poles in place of a pram, carried by two African servants. A later photograph shows him with his only playmate, a lion cub – there weren't many other young white children in Nairobi then.

David Roberts with my father, age ten months, 1913

My grandmother, I'm afraid to say, had become a bit of a snob and well aware of her new social standing in Nairobi. She decided that she wanted my grandfather to build them a house in what was to become the smartest place to live, Muthaiga – named after the bark from which the Maasai used to distil poison for their arrows. In 1912 they acquired twelve acres in this undeveloped area, where they planned to build a beautiful, large double storey house with walls made from quarry stone and a Mangalore tiled roof imported from India. It took many months to build this house, as the plot was covered in thick forest and the land had to be cleared by hand before any building could be started. There was no water or electricity supply in Muthaiga, but my grandparents were quite accustomed to living in houses without it, so neither of these problems deterred them in any way. Their house was certainly one of the first and finest properties to have been built in Muthaiga – double storey houses were unheard of then. It had long sweeping driveways with two sets of gates and almost as much land in the front of the house as there was at the back. How different this was from their first dwelling in Nairobi!

One of the only buildings in Muthaiga at that time was Homestead Farm – now Gertrude's Garden Children's hospital. It was owned by the Sandbach Baker family, who were given many acres of land by the British Government to facilitate the start of a dairy farm, which when established produced critically needed fresh dairy produce for the growing number of inhabitants in, and around Nairobi.

★

Pioneers were now employing numerous male servants to work in their homes, mainly from the Luo or Kikuyu tribes. It seems strange that they chose the men instead of the women as these men were used to hunting, looking after their goats and cows, or just sitting around talking while the women toiled. The men who worked in the houses were, condescendingly, referred to as 'houseboys' and are still called by that name, even by the wealthy black Kenyans who also now employ them.

House at Muthaiga c. 1914

Original house on the farm at Kiltannon, Kiambu

My grandfather with my father, 1912

My father with his elder brother, George, in the garden at Muthaiga

My father and his brother, George, at Muthaiga with the family servants

My grandparents employed a cook, three houseboys, including the faithful Owino, a *shamba (*gardener)*, a kitchen *toto* (child)*, a chauffeur and a male *Ayah* (nanny) for my father, all from the Luo tribe. The servants lived with their families in mud huts in a sectioned-off part of the garden. All their food such as sugar, tea, *posho*, meat and charcoal were provided by my grandparents, as was the custom in Kenya.

Afternoons were spent sitting in the shade of the veranda enjoying the sight of Sykes monkeys swinging in the avocado trees and the exotic African birds parading in the lush, colourful grounds. The gardens had quickly become established thanks to the wonderfully fertile, virgin African soil, and the loving care given to them by my grandmother and her *shamba*. They often entertained friends for tea, when Owino served finely cut cucumber sandwiches from bone china plates, while my grandmother poured tea from a crested silver teapot. After the servants had cleared the tea trolley away, they, and their friends, usually enjoyed a few games of tennis on the court, which they had later built at the bottom of the garden, before bathing and changing for dinner.

Every evening, with or without friends, my grandparents retired to their elegant drawing room, where at seven o'clock on the dot the trolley would again be wheeled in, this time laden with bottles of brandy, whisky and sherry, crystal glasses and a silver ice bucket. They enjoyed their evening drinks as they listened to the crickets and nocturnal animal grunts through the open doors. At eight o'clock sharp Granny rang her brass bell calling *"Lete chakula tafadhali"* indicating that it was time to serve the evening meal, while they poured themselves one last whisky and soda. Even if it was just the two of them, they sat in the dining room, the table set with a vase of waxy, sweet smelling, pink frangipani from the garden in the centre and the finest glass and silver. Most of the silver and china disappeared over the years due to breakages, theft or being dropped embarrassingly in front of guests by inebriated servants. Granny soon became wise to this and hiding what little sterling silver remained, had copies made locally from silver plate engraved with the family initials.

When serving guests, the servants added white gloves and a smart red waistcoat with gold braiding to the *kanzu* and red fez they usually wore. At least five courses were consumed, with sherry being served with the soup, white wine with the fish, red wine with the main course, sweet wine with the pudding and port with the cheese. A toast was made to the King before starting the meal, which usually lasted for several hours. The ladies disappeared to 'powder their noses' and have a good gossip in the main bedroom after dinner, before being served coffee and liqueurs in the drawing room. The men, having first 'visited Africa', a habit peculiar to male colonialists in Kenya, retired with their brandy and cigars to a timber room in the garden where Grandpa had installed a full size billiard table and comfortable leather chairs. The huge buffalo head, from the buffalo he had shot in 1900, loomed over the billiard table and the walls were adorned with photographs of his early days in Kenya. These tough pioneers sat in the 'billiard room', as we called it, for hours discussing politics and business, while the women chatted about fashion and caught up with the local gossip over coffee in the drawing room.

Having fun with a gramophone!

A cricket match -my grandparents at the front opposite Gladys and David Roberts, standing, Nairobi c. 1913

My grandmother was continually interested in who was building the latest house in Muthaiga, as for some reason she thought of Muthaiga as her private territory and was resentful of any new-comers. She often waited until she knew her neighbours were out before taking off with her chauffeur, and later also with me, a reluctant, but pliant accomplice, to inspect the new house. Once inside, my grandmother demanded their terrified servants to show her every room. The owners were invariably told about her visit on their return and were obviously furious, but they never dared to challenge her.

★

Gailey & Roberts was the first company to import motorcars and motorcycles to Kenya, although it is recorded that an early pioneer, George Wilson, imported a De Dion Bouton in 1903. He must have been quite crazy, as there were no petrol pumps, garages or spare parts, not to mention the lack of any roads to drive the car on! The situation was not a lot better when Grandpa 'caught the bug' and invested in his first motorcar, an Austin Hornsby, soon followed by a strange looking early motorcycle. He loved driving around Muthaiga in his motorcar, although he did not have the first idea how to operate it or how to cope with the mechanical side – luckily it was so slow that it didn't really matter. Despite owning two vehicles, my grandfather preferred to travel on horseback or by foot as he had done ever since he arrived in Africa, it was easier and faster. He eventually employed a chauffeur, not just to take my grandmother into Nairobi or to visit friends, but also to attend to the filthy job of lying under the vehicle in the red dust or swampy mud to maintain it. Not many people owned motorcars at this stage, but those who did, usually bought a Model T Ford, which was referred to locally as a 'Tin Lizzie'.

Inspecting the new motorcycle – my father trying on his father's' topi ,' with his brother, George, James Gailey, and my grandfather, Muthaiga

My grandfather in his first motorcar, an Austin Hornsby

At about the same time as my grandparents were building their house in Muthaiga, a group of pioneers, including my grandfather, were instrumental in starting the exclusive Muthaiga Country Club – usually referred to as 'The Muthaiga' by the members. The building was initially set in dusty barren acres which had been cleared from the thick surrounding forest and consisted of a long, low, brick, pebbledash building with Doric columns and airy open rooms leading off each other. The public rooms had dark woodblock floors and were furnished with heavy, comfy, floral upholstery. The early founders planted many colourful local trees and shrubs and it is thanks to them that the club is surrounded by beautiful lush gardens today. The Muthaiga Country Club opened its doors on 31 December 1913, providing a welcome meeting place for the local residents as well as for the farmers who lived 'up country'. The Club was strictly for members who had been carefully vetted by the committee before being allowed to join. Although always maintaining its exclusivity, it was unwittingly destined to become famous through many future scandals.

Muthaiga became a popular, but expensive place to live and settlers soon started building large private houses on spacious plots. Due to the influence of the local residents, at one time Muthaiga ended up with half the available electricity supply, leaving Nairobi and other areas with a huge problem. Electricity had reached central Nairobi in 1908, but was so unpredictable that instead of being called Nairobi Power and Lighting, the company became known locally as 'Nairobi Power and Darkness'.

There was huge rivalry between the Muthaiga Club and the Nairobi Club, which had been built slightly earlier, as members of the former considered that they were superior to the latter. This was mainly because many of them were aristocrats, settler farmers or they lived in Muthaiga, whereas The Nairobi Club was considered to be the domain of civil servants and the residents of Nairobi. As my grandfather was a founder member of both clubs, and had been a civil servant living in Nairobi, he felt equally at ease and loyal to each of them. He and my father remained members until they died.

Laying the foundation of the Muthaiga Country Club, 1912 – my grandmother, first on right, second row, my grandfather with moustache at the back.

A tea party at the Muthaiga Country Club, c. 1913

Shortly after the Muthaiga Club opened, many settlers, including my grandfather, arrived there by cart or on horseback eager to enlist and fight for England at the start of the First World War. Some joined what became the East African Mounted Rifles, and without any training or military leadership set off on horseback to the German East African border, eager to intercept the approaching German forces. They were armed in true pioneer spirit with only their hunting rifles, lances and a force of natives called the Carrier Corps. They had been recruited, not only to carry the ammunition and bedding on their heads, but also to lead the way through the hundreds of miles of thick forest and game tracks covered in 9ft. high elephant grass. Our brave young soldiers and their aides not only had to contend with the Germans, but also with the constant threat of marauding lions, herds of buffalo, rhino and other dangers. Illnesses such as black water fever and typhoid were another hazard as there were no doctors or hospitals anywhere near. It is amazing that most of them managed not only to survive, but helped to win the war. In some cases the soldiers were unaware that the war had ended until months after Armistice Day, as being in the middle of the bush they were completely out of touch with the rest of the world.

The war must have thrown my grandparents' lives into total disarray, as it did to so many others. I do not know where my grandmother and her two sons lived towards the end of the war, as their house became a nursing home for the wounded soldiers, as did the nearby newly opened Muthaiga Country Club. I only became aware that my grandparents' house had been requisitioned when I questioned my parents after I had woken to the sight of the ghostly apparition of a nurse, dressed as she would have been in 1914, standing by my bed – It was the only time I saw her.

CHAPTER EIGHT

THE RAMSAY BROTHERS

When George was fourteen and my father only seven, it was decided that they were to attend boarding schools in England, George at Dover College and my father at Yardley Court, before finishing his schooling at Tonbridge School in Kent. In 1920, my grandmother travelled to England with her sons to settle them into their new schools. They sailed on the *Guildford Castle*, a Union Castle Mail Steamship Company ship, arriving in Plymouth on 24 June 1920. She must have felt very sad on leaving her sons, knowing that it could be years before she saw them again.

My father (looking a bit tubby) with his aunts and uncle, Kent, 1927

It was not possible for the boys to travel back to Kenya for school holidays as travelling by ship took far too long. Consequently, they spent most of their holidays with their Uncle Arthur, my grandfather's unmarried brother, and his five unmarried aunts who all lived in a large house, 'Fiveways', situated in Scotts Lane, Shortlands, Bromley. Arthur, not surprisingly, escaped to the top floor where he became somewhat of a hermit. He lived an almost entirely separate life from that of his sisters who lived on the other floors of the house. Although George and my father became very attached to their uncle and aunts, they enjoyed spending some of their holidays with the Scales who lived in London. They had a son, Harold, who was about George's age and a daughter, Phoebe, who was the same age as my father. The four young friends enjoyed driving into the country for picnics and playing tennis at the local club. It was at this club that my parents were destined to meet and fall in love. The two families originally become friendly through their business connections, as Macdonald Scales was the British company used by Gailey & Roberts for the importation of farm machinery.

George found his senior school days particularly difficult as he had not received much of an education at the small school in Kenya run by the spinsters, but was expected to keep up with his peers at Dover College. Luckily he was good at sports, particularly hockey, and due to this and his affable character he was popular with both teachers and pupils. My father fared much better at Tonbridge School as he had started his schooling in England at a much earlier age, and he too excelled at all sports. Sadly, due to the difficulty in travelling to England after the war, it was six years before my grandparents saw their sons again. They arrived in Plymouth on 19 April 1926 on the *Armadale Castle* where they were noted as staying at 4 Chapel St. London. My grandfather calls himself a 'planter' on the ship's passenger list, probably because this was how most of the other passengers, being farmers in Kenya, had described themselves. My father had apparently changed so much that my grandparents had to ask one of the masters at the school to point him out to them on the rugby field.

On finishing at Dover College, George sailed back to Kenya ostensibly to work for Gailey & Roberts, but being a farmer at heart he soon became bored and attempted to start a farm with a friend, Lyle Shaw, at Koro. This venture was unfortunately unsuccessful and he decided to live on, and manage Grandpa's farm, Kiltannon, in Kiambu. Like most farmers, he constantly fought against locusts, drought and crop disease but still managed against all the odds to successfully continue growing coffee. Not long after George started managing Kiltannon, he was returning from a dance at the Kiambu Club when his car broke down on the dirt track compelling him to walk the last few miles home. He hadn't travelled very far before he was confronted by a large red eyed, belligerent bull buffalo which was far too close for comfort. Fortunately there was a gum tree nearby which he hastily climbed. However, the buffalo was in no hurry to move, forcing poor George to remain uncomfortably perched on a branch until dawn when the animal became bored and wandered off.

My grandfather with his sons, George and my father, Derek, Kent, 1927

George was good-looking, charming and socially in great demand. He had many female admirers and in 1934 he fell in love and married a beautiful society girl, Hazel Robinson, whom he had met at the Muthaiga Club. He took her to live with him on his farm, but it was a stormy marriage from the beginning as she enjoyed attending all the local parties while George was a hardworking farmer with little time for the social scene. After a few months,

63

Hazel left George in a blaze of publicity and scandal, which so horrified my grandparents that this marriage became a 'skeleton in the family cupboard'. All photographs of them together were destroyed and everyone involved at the time were sworn to secrecy. Hazel eventually left Nairobi, causing drama until the end. My grandmother decided to make amends by turning up at the Nairobi station armed with flowers, but she was met by hostile stares from Hazel and the friends who had assembled to wish her bon voyage. Hazel grabbed the flowers and threw them dramatically on the ground, before jumping on the train to Kitale where she made a new life for herself and was never mentioned in our family again.

CHAPTER NINE

A ROMANTIC MEETING

When my father ended his school days at Tonbridge he began training in London as an accountant, while living with our great family friends, the Scales, with whom he had spent so many happy school holidays. My father was very different in appearance to his brother, George, but equally handsome and popular with the girls, especially at the local tennis club where he was an excellent player. One day in 1933, he was introduced to my mother, a friend of Phoebe Scales's, who was to partner him at tennis in a game of mixed doubles. She was a beautiful, vivacious girl with pale skin, green eyes and thick auburn Pre-Raphaelite type hair. The attraction between them was instant and after that first meeting they knew they were meant for each other, or rather my mother did. She lived at 14 Bedford Close, Highgate, with my grandmother who was a widow and very protective of her only child.

My mother, Margaret Cecilia Coats, was born on 20 March 1913, the only child of Margaret Jane (nee Bentley) and George Coats, who had worked for more than forty-six years for the Northern and Allied Insurance Companies before retiring in December 1926. My mother was particularly close to her father and was devastated when he died on 14 August 1930 at the age of sixty-seven when she was only seventeen. I, of course, never met him, but am told that he had bright red hair and a red beard. He was born in Bo'Ness, near Edinburgh, the son of George Carrick Coats, who was born in New Brunswick, North America. He was the grandson of the founder of J&P Coats Ltd., of Paisley, Scotland (known as 'Coats Cotton'). Apparently, George Carrick Coats had become so sickened by all the family arguments over money and power that he decided to break away from his family and their business, forfeiting his huge inheritance. When he was twenty-five years old he returned to Scotland with his mother, Elizabeth, and his share of the family silver. He became a Collector of Customs for Scotland and England.

My maternal grandmother, Gagee, was born at Hill Farm, Driffield, Yorkshire, one of nine children. She trained as a nurse, working for many years in the children's ward at Castle Tree House Hospital in Lincoln. Her favourite sister, Harriet, was a cook, one of twelve servants working for the family who owned Watton Grange in Watton, Yorkshire. She was very attractive and ended up marrying the eldest son, Dixon Nicholson, and became the mistress of Watton Grange. My mother spent many happy holidays visiting her cousins and often talked of her love for Yorkshire.

My parents met secretly as often as they could, at the tennis club or in central London where my father was completing his accountancy training. My mother, following in her father's footsteps, worked as a secretary in the same company he had worked in for so many years, the Northern and Allied Insurance Companies. My father accompanied her home most evenings by bus, but disappeared into the bushes as soon as the maid opened the front door. For some reason it was many months before my mother plucked up the courage to introduce him to her mother, probably because she knew she may be leaving her alone in England if he eventually asked her to marry him. On 15 April 1933, my paternal grandmother, Alice, arrived from Mombasa on the on the SS *Maida*, a British Indian Steam Navigation Company ship (known locally as B.I.) to accompany my father on the Grand Tour, therefore, he and my mother were separated for many weeks. They missed each other terribly, my mother probably more than my father at that stage, but he kept in touch by sending her postcards from every port of call.

My mother was extremely upset when it was decided that my father was to stop training as an accountant in London and return to Kenya with his mother to work for Gailey & Roberts. However, my father was thrilled, as although he was born in Nairobi, he had not been back since leaving to attend Yardley Court in Kent at the age of seven. In one letter written to my mother from the ship taking him and his mother back to Kenya, he rather arrogantly writes: "There is no one I particularly like on this boat, and most of the girls on board are engaged, so all goes well for us so far." This must have hurt and concerned my mother who was desperate to marry him, but he was obviously not in any hurry at all. They corresponded for eighteen months, the letters becoming more and more loving, but there was no mention of marriage. Eventually, having not had any luck on board ship, and no doubt having romanced every attractive available girl in Kenya, my father decided that it was my mother he loved and wanted to spend the rest of his life with.

The much longed-for letter arrived in August asking my mother if she would agree to marry him and make a new life in East Africa. This was a huge step for her, as it meant leaving her mother, whom she adored, and all her friends to live in some far-off place of which she had hardly heard. She hadn't even met her future parents-in-law, but her love for my father was so strong that she accepted his proposal without hesitation. Gagee was naturally apprehensive at the thought of her daughter marrying a man whom she hardly knew, and my mother was concerned about deserting her. However, my grandparents, being generous-hearted people, suggested that Gagee should also come to live in Nairobi, promising that they would provide her with a house near her daughter and future son-in-law. Much as she dreaded the thought of being parted from her daughter, Gagee was not easily persuaded. However, eventually it was agreed that my mother would sail back to England once she had settled in Kenya to accompany her back to her new home in Nairobi. Neither of them could possibly have foreseen that when my mother returned, London would be in turmoil and their lives in great danger.

★

My grandparents were delighted that their younger son was getting married and my grandmother immediately started to plan a large wedding. The guest list included most of the early pioneers and the cream of Kenya society. The two bridesmaids were daughters of friends, and the bride was to be given away by my grandparents' best friend and business partner, James Gailey. Granny thoroughly enjoyed organizing every little detail of what was to become the 'wedding of the year' according to 'Miranda's Merrier Moments', a weekly society column featured in the *East African Standard*. The identity of the writer of this page was always kept a secret, although she miraculously managed to attend every single social occasion. We eventually discovered there were several 'Mirandas' and one of them much later became a great friend of my mother's.

CHAPTER TEN

A KENYA WEDDING

My Mother, Margaret Cecilia Coats, sailed into the port of Mombasa on the *SS Madura* complete with an oyster silk wedding dress packed in tissue paper, a coronet of mother-of-pearl orange blossom and a fashionable trousseau. She thoroughly enjoyed the voyage, as travelling alone and being young, vivacious and beautiful had many admirers. She was the centre of attention throughout and made many lifelong friendships on that maiden voyage.

The marriage took place within a few days of my mother's arrival in Nairobi on 19 December 1936 at the Nairobi Cathedral. Sadly, none of her own family or friends were able to attend the wedding and it was the first time she had met her parents-in-law, her three bridesmaids, the best man, Jack Block, or any of the guests. As Pam (the daughter of my grandmother's sister, Daisy) had unexpectedly arrived back from England, it was decided at the last minute that she should become the third bridesmaid, a matching dress being hastily run up for her by a local Indian tailor. Although Pam had been born in Kenya, she had been educated in England and therefore did not know any of the wedding guests either, consequently she and my mother became instant friends. The reception was held on the lawns of my grandparents' house in Muthaiga where tables seating eight guests, covered in white antique lace-edged cloths, were scattered randomly under the trees. The happy, smiling servants dressed in their smartest *kanzus,* red waistcoats and white gloves served champagne and canapés to the guests. They loved these special occasions and they were always thanked after the event with extra large pay packets.

My Parents' Wedding, 19 December 1936

'Miranda's Merrier Moments' described the bride's dress as being:

A gown of oyster 'charmeuse' with a silver lamé thread, cut with a draped cowl neckline, small basque, long tight sleeves with epaulettes at the corners, with a silver girdle at the waist. Silver leaves surmounted the bride's net veil, and she carried a sheaf of lilies. Her chief bridesmaid, Joan Pottinger, wore white embroidered organdie over a white satin slip, with leaves of organdie at the neck in front, and a low square neckline at the back. A 'Dolly Varden' headdress of English wild flowers set on white frilled organdie completed the ensemble. The other two bridesmaids, Pam Riley and Audrey Gregory wore white organdie dresses with very large puff sleeves and enormous sashes of organdie, with headdresses of leaves. They all carried bouquets of love-in-the-mist and delphiniums. The groom's mother, Alice Ramsay, wore a beige lace outfit and a Bangkok straw hat trimmed with dark brown ribbon.

My grandparents' wedding present to the young couple was a newly built stone bungalow, situated opposite the Nairobi Club in the area formally called Railway Hill, now commonly known as 'The Hill'. This was the same plot of land that had housed the tiny timber and iron house my grandparents had once lived in, which was to be given to Gagee when she arrived from England. The plot had been divided in two, giving each house a generous acre of land. The new bungalow had an enormous drawing room with parquet floors, separate dining room and the mandatory veranda. The kitchen and pantries were spacious and four bedrooms led off a long passage which was open on one side, but protected by ornate steel bars. The house was completely designed, decorated and fully furnished by my grandmother using furniture which had been made locally out of wood from the muvulia tree.

The honeymoon was also arranged and paid for by my grandparents. Their surprise destination was a lovely hotel, The Wilderness, near the awe-inspiring Murchison Falls in Uganda. My parents loved Uganda, promising that they would spend many future holidays there, but for some reason they never went back. On returning from their honeymoon they settled happily into their new home in Nairobi. My mother, although appreciative of the wonderful wedding present her parents-in-law had given them, was rather peeved that she had not been allowed to at least choose her own furnishings and décor. Not being used to having servants she found it rather intimidating having to deal with so many of them, who didn't speak any English and had all been chosen and employed by my grandmother. However, she soon learned to speak basic 'pidgin' Swahili and enjoyed trying out new recipes with her *mpishi*, as well as working in the garden with her shamba. The word 'shamba' actually means smallholding in Swahili, but the settlers usually called their gardeners by that name. It amazed my mother how the African servants responded to everything with such willingness and how readily they learnt the etiquette of the British middle classes, which must have seemed so utterly ridiculous to them. They accepted unreasonable demands from frustrated and often bad tempered memsahibs, as they struggled to teach their staff how to set out the silver and prepare a chocolate mousse. Whatever was demanded of them, they responded with a smiling face, nothing was too much trouble. The *mpishis* quickly learnt how to prepare wonderful dishes and to cope admirably with the smartest of large dinner parties, often with very little notice.

The houseboys spent every morning cleaning the house, whizzing happily up and down the floors with sheepskin cloths tied to their feet as they polished the parquet to perfection. They cleaned the silver so enthusiastically, with a product that looked like Vim, that over the years the hallmarks became almost obliterated. At meal times they served the food and wines as expertly as any silver service waiter from a top London restaurant, even if it was just for the family. The shambas, under the supervision of the memsahibs, using colourful local plants and trees such as cannas, bougainvillea, jacaranda and frangipani, mixed with English roses and fuchsia, created the most beautiful, lush gardens out of the fertile red soil. They didn't have such a thing as a lawnmower, but cut the strong green Kikuyu grass with a *panga*, which is similar to a crude very sharp machete. These pangas were used by the natives for just about everything from cutting wood to killing and skinning animals, and during the Mau Mau uprising hacking people to death. My parents' servants lived with their families in mud and wattle houses in a compound in the garden which was separated from the main house by a hedge – I will never forget the wonderful intoxicating smell of the acrid wood smoke constantly in the air from their cooking fires.

Shopping for provisions in Nairobi was another huge challenge my mother had to overcome, as there were no clean, friendly corner shops such as she had been used to in Highgate. Instead, she learnt to fight her way round the filthy, bustling, local market where an assortment of colourful mangoes, sweet potatoes, tiny bananas and some wilting green vegetables were spread out on the floor next to different cuts of meat covered in flies and rotting in the sun.

Bread, milk and imported tinned products were purchased from the nearby open-fronted Indian *dukas*. All vegetables and fruit, once purchased, were washed in a bath of purple potassium permanganate to kill any parasites and the meat was well cooked to guard against the dreaded tapeworm.

Other unpleasant experiences were the swarms of huge locusts which arrived in a thick black cloud ruining farmer's crops and clinging to people's clothes and skin in a frightening way. Then there were the flying ants, which after the long rains poured into the house through open windows and doors in their droves, transparent wings vibrating wildly. Bodies and wings littered every floor, before the servants swept them up in heaps, often to be eaten by them later as a tasty treat.

★

My mother soon took a job as a secretary for the Special Branch of the Kenya Police Force, while my father worked for Gailey & Roberts in Nairobi. The company had gone from strength to strength over the years and by 1925 had spread its wings, boasting five branches situated all over the country. Towards the end of 1937, it was suggested that my father should become much more involved in the company, with a view to taking over his father's role as Managing Director, as James Gailey was ill and Grandpa wanted to retire. However, my father did not feel that he had enough experience to handle so much responsibility at his young age, especially as he had spent such a short time working for the company, and turned the offer down. This must have been a great disappointment to James Gailey and my grandfather. I'm sure he hoped that at least one of his sons would follow in his footsteps, and George was managing the farm at Kiambu. After much discussion between my family and the Gaileys it was decided to sell Gailey and Roberts Ltd., to The United Africa Company, which was owned by Unilever, and the sale was completed within the same year. My grandfather retained shares in the company and it is recorded that he remained Chairman in a non-executive capacity until he died in 1953. In 1997 The United Africa Company sold Gailey & Roberts to the Egyptian Caterpillar dealer, Mantrac, which was owned by the Mansour Group. They are still active today with many branches throughout Kenya and Uganda.

The Gaileys lived on their coffee farm, 'Ngewe', in Ruiru, not far from Kiambu. Gladys died on 9 July 1946 and surprisingly is buried next to her first husband, David Roberts, in the Nairobi South Cemetery. I can find no official record of James Gailey's death, or the place where he was buried or cremated. However, he became a member of the Donyo Sabuk Freemason Lodge in 1927 where his death is recorded as being on 1 August 1938. He left all his money to his sister, Lavender, who lived in England, in trust for my father and his elder brother, George. Lavender lived until she was nearly a hundred and the two brothers did not inherit until about 1963. There was inevitably some dispute with the Gaileys' distant relatives who felt they should have inherited, but this was resolved amicably.

Meanwhile my parents became involved in the active social scene in, and around, the Nairobi Club, with my father spending most evenings and weekends playing tennis and squash, while my mother occasionally enjoyed a quieter game of tennis in the afternoons with her girlfriends. There were lunch or dinner parties held at friends' houses and dances held at the Nairobi Club or the Norfolk Hotel at every opportunity.

My Mother, somehow, found time soon after her marriage to visit her mother in England, taking a flying boat from Lake Naivasha, which was used as a staging post by the Imperial Airways flying boat services to Southampton. These flying boats were fixed-winged seaplanes with a hull, allowing them to land on water and, as can be imagined, there was great excitement when they first arrived at Naivasha. They accommodated about twenty passengers, and the ground and flight deck crew were all males, which would have appealed to my mother! They stopped at many interesting places including Durban, Rome, Athens and Alexandria.

On 15 May 1939, at the beginning of the Second World War my mother arrived in Plymouth on the *Llangibby Castle* to accompany Gagee back to her new home in Nairobi. It was a frightening time for them, as by the time she had helped her mother pack up the family house in Highgate the war was well under way. It was extremely difficult and dangerous to get back to Kenya as U-boats were slinking, menacingly and silently under the sea searching for their prey, and passenger ships, despite being painted grey, were particularly targeted. They eventually managed to wangle a first class cabin on a Blue Funnel Line ship, the *Anchises* sailing on 27 September. Everybody on board was aware they could be torpedoed or bombed at any moment, invoking a feeling of camaraderie with the general motto on board being 'lets live every minute as if our last' as more life-long friendships were made. Fortunately the ship arrived safely in Mombasa or I would not be here to tell the tale!

★

Gagee moved into the little wooden house on stilts with a tin roof, next door to my parents, and quickly settled into life in Africa. She struck up an immediate friendship with Daisy, Granny's widowed sister, and they became such good friends that Daisy eventually moved into Gagee's house where they lived happily together for many years.

After my father, I was the second baby in our family to be born in Kenya, on 11 November 1940 at the Maia Carberry Hospital in Nairobi. My grandparents were delighted to have a granddaughter, although Granny was horrified that I had been born with bright red hair. It was a great comfort for my mother to have her mother, Gagee, living next door, especially when my father joined the King's African Rifles and was posted to Abyssinia to fight the Italians, leaving her to cope with a small baby. My father's cousin, Pam, came to live with my mother for a short time as they both worked in Nairobi, Pam in the Standard Bank and my mother still with the Special Branch of the Kenya Police Force. Despite my mother being married with a child, the two attractive young women had a wonderful time being wined, dined and spoiled with silk stockings, bunches of violets and chocolates by the young British soldiers who were based in Nairobi. We were all issued with gas masks and a bunker was dug in the garden, which we children later found was great fun to play in. Although our men were risking their lives fighting, the war didn't affect us as it did our friends in England, as there was always plenty of food and Nairobi, thankfully, was never bombed.

Pam soon fell in love with a Scotsman, Robert Stanley Harris, known as Stan, who worked with her in the Standard Bank in Nairobi. They were married on 17 May 1942 in a church in Parklands, with my mother as Maid of Honour and the reception held on the lawns of my grandparents' house in Muthaiga. In 1945 Pam and Stanley produced a daughter whom they named Elaine, who was later educated at The Loreto Convent in Nairobi. In 1950 they had another daughter, Claire, who was educated in Scotland and spent most holidays with my grandmother's other sister, Kitty and her family.

The flying-boat on Lake Naivasha

Gagee's House in Nairobi

CHAPTER ELEVEN

HAPPY VALLEY

In July 1920, British East Africa became a Crown Colony, and in 1922 the local currency was changed from the East African Rupee to the Kenya Shilling. Kenya was expanding fast with new businesses, shops, hotels and farms sprouting up everywhere. By the 1930s it was also becoming a fashionable place to live, with many aristocrats seduced by the 'promised land' investing in the beautiful cedar-forested foothills of the Aberdares. Some became farmers and others went into politics or started businesses. Most were diligent and sincere, but a few had loose morals, plenty of cash and did nothing much with their time except enjoy an excessively hedonistic existence.

Some of the wealthier new arrivals chose to buy vast acres of lush green land in the idyllic mystical area around the Wanjohi River, more than 6,000 feet above sea level, where they planned to farm the land. They built smart homes and employed proud and elegant male Somali servants, who were often exploited by them, to answer to their every whim. Parties were held in different houses from dawn to dusk, with the guests enjoying pink gins at midday and strange potent cocktails in the evening. Cocaine and opium were used in abundance and promiscuity was de rigueur. The men often wore silk pyjamas, smoking jackets and cravats, while the ladies vied for attention in elaborate evening gowns or floppy, silk trousers worn with rows of valuable pearls. Lady Idina Hay, as she was then, was renowned for greeting her guests at her home, Slains, while still naked in the bath sipping champagne. She also enjoyed playing a bizarre after-dinner game, which involved the male guests sticking part of their anatomy through holes in a sheet so the women could have their choice – they all loved this game! They became known as the infamous Happy Valley set. I think it would be more accurate to describe them as the 'Unhappy Valley set' as it seems to me that they were only happy when high on drugs, alcohol and sex, but in reality they were a rather spoilt and not very happy group of misfits. What on earth did the proud Somali servants think of it all?

My parents were certainly not part of this 'set', although they were friendly with most of the people who were involved, as they met them at the Muthaiga Club. My mother often talked of the evening they had been invited to supper by a married couple who lived in Karen, and who later turned out to be prominent members of the Happy Valley set. On arriving at the house, their hosts were nowhere to be seen. My parents were rather surprised to be greeted by the nanny, who took them to a separate building in the garden to introduce them to the host's children. On returning to the main house, they were ushered into the drawing room by a Somali servant wearing white gloves and embroidered velvet slippers. He prepared a cocktail for them, but there was still no sign of anyone. Eventually, various bedroom doors started to open and the hosts and their guests appeared, totally inebriated, on the arms of each other's spouses or partners. All this horrified my parents who at the time had no idea that such decadence was occurring in Kenya.

★

The main social events of the year were still the bi-annual race meetings held in Nairobi, when hard working farmers and the Happy Valley set travelled from their remote farms to stay at the Muthaiga Club or the Norfolk Hotel. There were nightly balls at the club, which usually turned into debauched, drunken brawls with furniture being flung out of the windows and bread rolls thrown around the dining room. The Prince of Wales (later Edward V111) and his younger brothers, Prince George, the Duke of Kent and Prince Henry, the Duke of Gloucester, loved staying at the Muthaiga Club during their frequent hunting visits to Kenya. It is rumoured that Prince George's long-time glamorous, but drug addicted, American girl friend, Alice 'Kikki' Gwynne, was pregnant by him but it was never proved whether or not she actually had the baby.

There was also much speculation that one of Prince Henry's mistresses, Beryl Markham, (the first woman to fly solo from England to America, and also a member of the Happy Valley set) had produced two babies by him, before being paid-off by Queen Mary. A much repeated story is that aided and abetted by a local beauty, Lady Erskine, the Prince of Wales once swung on the chandeliers in the ballroom of the Muthaiga Club, before throwing all the records out of the windows because he disliked the music. These unruly occasions usually continued in the early hours when some of the more boisterous partygoers drove rickshaws into Nairobi where they took pot shots at everything in sight, including the street lamps. They usually ended up at the Norfolk Hotel, the infamous Long Bar at the New Stanley or Torrs Hotel, referred to locally as 'Tarts' Hotel', where they continued causing havoc well into the next day.

★

Many books have been written about the murder of Josslyn Hay, Earl of Erroll, whose body was discovered on 24 January 1941 at about three o'clock in the morning, slumped and bloody with a bullet through his head, lying on the floor of his Buick on the Ngong road, eight miles from Nairobi. Lord Erroll was now single, having divorced Idina and his second wife, Molly (who died of drugs and alcohol poisoning) and had recently been appointed Military Secretary – he was also a member of the Happy Valley set. Due to his exceptional good looks, charm and impressive title he was irresistible to women. At one stage, when he was married to Molly, he owned a palatial house on the shores of Lake Naivasha, Oserian, known locally as the 'Djinn Palace', where he conducted numerous love affairs, particularly with married women. There was much speculation among the local community as to who had killed Lord Erroll, as there is today – had he been murdered by a jealous husband, a spurned lover or even by MI5 as he was heavily into politics and pro Oswald Mosley? There were also claims that he was a Nazi supporter and collaborated with the Germans during the war, and that he was part of a renegade group which included Rudolph Hess and the Duke of Windsor.

The news of his murder instantly made worldwide headlines and Kenya became famous overnight for all the wrong reasons. Most of the hardworking inhabitants were horrified by the scandalous stories detailing the indolent and promiscuous lives led by the Happy Valley set which were revealed daily in the newspapers. There was huge controversy as to who had shot Lord Erroll, who, at the time of the murder had been having a very public affair with the blonde and beautiful Diana Broughton (later to become Lady Delamere). On the night of the murder he was returning to his rented house in Muthaiga having taken Diana home after wining and dining her at the Muthaiga Club. Suspicion immediately fell on Diana's much older husband, Sir Henry 'Jock' Delves Broughton, despite the fact that he appeared to condone his wife's philandering, and he went on trial at the wood-panelled Nairobi Law Courts on 26 May 1941. My mother often talked about how she and her friends enjoyed this diversion from the seriousness of the war, and 'dressed up to the nines' attended the daily court proceedings with great interest. They, of course, knew most of the witnesses who were all colourful characters in their own way, and I grew up meeting most of them. I recall sitting next to Beryl Markham at a dinner party many years later and finding her, disappointingly, withdrawn and rather boring. However, my parents, who had known her for years, described her as avant-garde, vivacious, beautiful and fearless, but she had loose morals and was conducting numerous affairs with different men at the same time as her dalliance with Prince Henry.

The beautiful, but mad, Countess Alice de Janze, apart from injecting herself with heroin, was known to have a great love for animals. She was inseparable from her pet lion cub, Samson, apparently, on one occasion travelling to England with him and keeping him in her London flat. Alice later divorced her husband and married her lover, Raymund de Trafford, whom she had earlier famously shot in a display of *crime passionnel* at the Gare du Nord in Paris, before turning the gun on herself. They both survived, but their marriage did not and they were divorced within three months.

June and John Carberry were a strange couple. She was a pretty woman who chain- smoked, with a brandy and water constantly by her side, but was faithful to Diana and Delves Broughton to the end. My mother was fond of June as she was amusing and warm hearted and they became good friends. She was certain June knew who had murdered Lord Erroll as she was at the house with Diana at the time, but if she did, she took the secret with her to the grave. Her mean-faced husband, John, was a sadistic drunk who was extremely cruel to his only daughter and was universally disliked. Lady Idina, now married to her fifth husband, William Vincent Soltau, was an intelligent, plain, promiscuous woman who was irresistible to men, but the person everyone was really interested in was Diana Broughton. She was invariably portrayed as being ethereally beautiful, but my mother always thought that she had a hard expressionless face and was 'a bit common'.

This intriguing court case attracted an audience from all over Kenya and beyond, with people queuing for a place in the stifling hot courtroom from the crack of dawn. Farmers and their wives travelled to Nairobi from their estates 'up country' filling the clubs and hotels to capacity, with all eyes fixed on the flamboyant and by now infamous witnesses. Diana Broughton stunned the gallery on the first day of the trial by appearing dressed in black and dripping in diamonds. From then on she wore rows of pearls and a different stylish and expensive outfit every day. Newspaper reporters from all over the world arrived in Nairobi to report on this extraordinary murder trial. Apart from the atmosphere being charged with excitement and anticipation at the thought of Delves Broughton possibly being the first white person to be hanged in Kenya, the trial attracted so much attention because it involved the aristocracy and the scene was set in the glorious landscape of Africa. For years after this scandal people would ask: "Are you married, or do you live in Kenya?"

Inspector Arthur Poppy, who was a friend of my mother's as they worked together in the Special Branch of the Kenya Police Force, was in charge of the investigation. He had the impossible task of questioning the Happy Valley set, who closed ranks, refused to disclose any information they may have had and gave alibis for each other. It is, of course, also possible that they were all too drugged or drunk to remember anything that had occurred on that fateful night. Although the Inspector did not discuss the case with her, he apparently remarked to my mother that he was receiving anonymous letters naming the murderer, and it wasn't Delves Broughton. After twenty-seven days Sir Henry 'Jock' Delves Broughton was sensationally acquitted in what was largely regarded as a blatant miscarriage of justice, but no proof was found to convict him. He took an overdose less than a year later in his room at the Adelphi Hotel in Liverpool. His suicide was, reportedly, more likely to have been due to financial problems that he was having at the time than the possibility that he had murdered his wife's lover.

Strangely, Alice de Trafford, as she was by then, also committed suicide soon after Lord Erroll's murder and it was my parents' handsome doctor, Doctor William Boyle, an ex lover of Alice's, who was called to the scene. She was found lying on her bed, surrounded by flowers, with her head swathed in yards of chiffon.

It is said that there were people who knew who the murderer was, but as most of them are now dead, the secret has died with them. I have often thought my mother must have known more than she admitted because of her job and friendship with Arthur Poppy, but if she did, as with many others, she kept silent. A film, White Mischief, has since been made about this case, books have been written by investigative authors and unreliable professed witnesses, and secret tapes naming Delves Broughton as the killer have apparently been found. I believe that no one will ever know, or want to know, for certain who the murderer in this enthralling case really was and that the murder of Lord Erroll will forever remain a mystery.

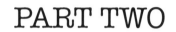

PART TWO

CHAPTER ONE

MY EARLY CHILDHOOD

Although I did not always fully appreciate it, I was very blessed to be born and brought up in Africa with its vast breathtaking landscapes, incredible feeling of space and privileged lifestyle. How lucky I was as a child to be lulled to sleep every night to the rhythmic beating of the African drums in the distance and the ebony sky bejewelled with glittering stars outside my open window. It was quite normal to hear the growl of a leopard or the eerie laugh of the hyenas scavenging outside our house at night, and because I was accustomed to these noises I found them rather comforting. Hyenas are the most reviled creatures in Africa, as apart from being predators, they are extremely ugly and are associated with evil witchcraft in some cultures. I doubt many people would enjoy hearing them outside their window at night as I did!

How lucky I was to wake up to the smells of Africa, the earth so red, the sun so brilliant and the flowers so colourful. Each new day for my family began with our faithful houseboy, Odawa, quietly knocking on the bedroom doors with the words "*Hodi, memsahib, chai.*" He then appeared, grinning from ear to ear, with trays containing cups, saucers and pots of strong Kenya tea for every bedroom. In whichever country I have since lived, I have found it difficult to start the day without this very colonial custom. In England it is now my husband who kindly brings me a tray of tea and not Odawa! Breakfast was a family affair as we sat around the dining room table contemplating the day ahead, while being served pawpaw and limes from our garden, usually followed by porridge, toast, marmalade and fresh coffee from Kiltannon, the family farm in Kiambu.

My earliest memories are mainly of my grandmother, Gagee. I adored her, and she was definitely the pivotal person throughout my early life. She had married quite late, and for many years before her marriage had been a dedicated nursing sister working in a hospital for underprivileged children in Lincoln. I still have photos showing her in a hospital ward where three or more sick children shared the same simple cots. She was a down-to-earth sensible Yorkshire woman which I always found so comforting.

Gagee, Nairobi, 1942

Me with my father, Nairobi, 1942

I was born in the low stone house on 'The Hill' opposite the Nairobi Club, which had been given to my parents as a wedding present by my grandparents. Gagee lived next door to us in the little wood and tin house on stilts with a veranda running the length of it, where my grandparents had once lived. It was separated from our house by a scruffy old plumbago hedge which I could easily crawl through for my daily visits. I loved listening to Gagee reading poetry to me from her much loved leather bound collection of Keats, Robert Browning and Shelley while we sat under a gnarled old pepper tree. Sometimes we picked flowers from her pretty little garden, preserving them by pressing them between the pages of her favourite poems. Many hours were spent making clothes out of an assortment of odd scraps for my only doll, my beloved rag doll, Rosie. During the war there were no toys available to buy in Kenya, or if there were I certainly didn't have any, and neither did I need them when I had my wonderful grandmother for company.

When I was four years old I was sent to a nursery school, Coconuts, which was situated in a large corrugated-shed on stilts. It was owned and run by Miss Vetch, a jolly spinster with bright red hair. By eleven o'clock, we children had usually become so hot that we were forced to spend the rest of the day playing and eating our lunch on the red earth under the floor of the shed. I was a rather greedy child and I recall pretending to help the younger children unpack their lunch boxes, but eating most of their food myself. I was very happy there, but Miss Vetch was not so enamoured with me, as soon after my arrival the metal tonic bottle tops, which were used as counters, started slowly disappearing. It was eventually discovered that for some inexplicable reason I was filling my knickers with them every day, taking them home and hiding them in my room. I later attended Parklands School, which I do not remember much about, and thereafter I was sent to the Loreto Convent in Nairobi. The nuns seemed much kinder to the Catholic girls than they were to us Protestants, and I remember trying to persuade them that I was really a Roman Catholic and it was my parents who were Protestants, but of course they never believed me.

★

The first time I remember seeing my father was when he came home at the end of the war, and my mother told me that someone called 'Daddy' was coming to live with us permanently. I was not too happy about this as I liked having my mother to myself. I had been used to kind 'uncles' popping in for a drink or a meal, bringing me a present and a bunch of violets for my mother, then going away, but this 'Daddy' was going to be living with us all the time! However when he arrived, tanned, good-looking and armed with a blue cane pram for my rag doll, Rosie, I quickly thawed and decided to accept him.

When I was older, my grandmother, Alice, occasionally arrived in her car, complete with her smartly dressed African chauffeur, to collect me from school. I loved spending the day with my grandparents at their house in Muthaiga as they treated me with great respect and not like a child at all. The three of us enjoyed lunch, sitting at the table with the inevitable vase of waxy frangipani from the garden in the centre, with the meal served by their happy, smiling servants. It was at times like this, even as a small child, that I was fascinated to hear my grandparents reminiscing about their early lives as pioneers in Kenya. Granny was by then rather dumpy with short grey hair. She was always smartly dressed, mainly in black and white, and I never saw her without a handbag made of jingly black beads. Grandpa was a large, kindly, quiet man who often wore a topi and always had a pipe in his hand. I don't remember Granny having many female friends, but Grandpa spent endless hours reminiscing or playing billiards with his old cronies. My grandparents often took me to rather adult films which were showing at the newly opened Capital Cinema, where women wore their best dresses and the men wore dinner jackets regardless of the heat. When I was six years old I was taken to a very romantic and probably most unsuitable film, *Blue Lagoon,* which I loved and have never forgotten.

My grandparents, George and Alice Ramsay, 1943

My mother, 1943

Every Sunday afternoon the whole family visited my grandparents at their house in Muthaiga for tea, but ended up staying until well after the drinks-trolley had been wheeled in at seven o'clock – you could set the clock by that drinks-trolley. For some reason they never turned the lights on until it was completely dark. It never ceased to fascinate me how we sat in the drawing room, the adults sipping their whisky and soda while discussing politics or family finances in almost complete darkness. The house was dark anyway as the walls of the hall and stairways were all painted black, maybe it was the fashion then. Granny ensured that I was not bored on these weekly visits by unfailingly producing some sweets and a surprise present. The present was usually something educational, such as a book of different flags for me to cut out and paste in the correct countries, or on another occasion, a globe.

★

My mother was undoubtedly in awe of my grandmother, and I believe she found her rather stiff and formal. Although I never saw that side of her, I can imagine some people may have thought her rather formidable, especially a daughter-in-law. My mother became extremely annoyed when on returning from a holiday on a couple of occasions, we found that Granny had completely redecorated our house as a surprise. It was not a very happy surprise for my mother, as she never approved of the colour of the paint that had been chosen.

I was aware even as a child that my mother was very attractive, vivacious and popular, not only from the way men looked at her when she entered a room, but also how other women regarded her. She had the precious gift of making anyone she was talking to feel as if they were the most interesting and important person in the room. She was also a terrible flirt and enjoyed nothing more than being constantly surrounded by admiring men. It never seemed to concern my father that on her birthdays she received unsigned cards from various admirers, some of which I have kept. They read:

"To Ravishing Ramsay – my glass I raise, full of bubbles, to happy days free from troubles" – "To Marvelous Margaret" – "To Beauty from The Beast", and a further one, "To scintillating Celia" – her middle name was Cecilia.

My mother was devoted to my father, as he was to her, and I am certain she was never unfaithful to him despite living in Kenya during the Happy Valley era. They loved entertaining and I remember once being horrified to see a well known, short and very fat judge's wife shimmying down the stairs in nothing but a corset at one of their lunch parties! They attended almost nightly dinners at friends' houses, dances at the Muthaiga Club and evenings at the Donovan Maule or National Theatre. My mother never forgot to tuck me up in bed at night, elegantly dressed and smelling of Chanel No. 5, before disappearing with my father into the dark African night.

CHAPTER TWO

GROWING UP IN KENYA

I considered my father handsome, which he undeniably was, with the demeanour and steady gaze of an honest, confident man, although in some ways he was rather distant with me, almost as if he wasn't quite sure how a father should behave. I never remember him giving me a hug or cuddle, and this is probably because he had never received any demonstrative affection from his parents. He was an excellent sportsman and played competitive tennis or squash at the Nairobi Club every afternoon. He returned from the Club at seven o'clock, dressed in white sports attire. He never changed, but immediately collapsed on the sofa with his pipe and a whisky and soda by his side. My mother invariably questioned him about the different women he had played mixed doubles with that afternoon, and whether he had taken them for a drink in the bar before coming home. I think she was rather envious of these women tennis players, although she generally had an admirer or two of her own to keep her company while she took afternoon tea on the veranda. These men were usually lonely divorcees or widowers and I am sure it was all very innocent, but I disliked them as I wanted to spend that precious time alone with my mother.

Instead, I spent the afternoons with my nanny, playing on the swings with other children on the sports grounds of the Nairobi Club. I longed for the moment when we heard the sounds of the bugle from the nearby army headquarters playing the Last Post and the Union Jack was lowered at sunset, as this meant that it was time to go home for supper. This normally consisted of steamed cow's brains and vegetables followed by junket or jelly. I thoroughly disliked this nursery food, but pretended that I enjoyed it as this was my chance to be alone with my mother. She unfailingly made a point of sitting at the table in the kitchen and chatting to me while I ate. At night I slept with strands of my hair wound round my father's pipe cleaners, which were used as curlers, so that everyone thought that I had curly hair when in fact it was completely straight. When my hair grew longer I was spared this indignity and eventually wore it in long heavy plaits down to my waist. Every year my grandparents held lavish birthday parties for me in the beautiful gardens of their home in Muthaiga, complete with a hired merry-go-round, ponies and magicians. I enjoyed being the centre of attention in my best lace party dress and receiving lovely imported gifts, but I usually ended up having a tantrum which was put down to me being over-tired.

In later years I was reminded of the times when my mother's friends dropped their children at our house for afternoon tea, but quickly getting bored of playing with them, I locked them in the lavatory until it was time for them to go home – I don't think I was a very pleasant child!

★

On 9 October 1945, I was given a brother, Kevin Allen, a large beautiful baby who immediately took all my mother's love and attention. This catastrophe pushed me even closer to my grandparents, especially Gagee who was not particularly interested in this golden boy either. Despite my original negative feelings, I eventually became very protective and loving towards this new intruder, but sadly in later years we became forever estranged.

In that same year, George, my father's brother, brought his attractive new Scottish wife, Elizabeth (nee Anderson), to meet the family. He had proposed to her in Mauritius during the war while she was working for the British Foreign Office and he was in the Royal Artillery. George desperately wanted to join the Navy and at the start of the war, when he happened to be in London, eagerly attempted to sign up at the War Office only to be told that he was too old. Disappointed, he returned to Kenya where he joined the King's African Rifles and like my father was sent to Abyssinia to fight the Italians. He was later commissioned in the Royal Artillery where he spent his time mainly in the coastal regions, before being sent by sea to join his regiment in Madagascar. It was on this voyage that he met and fell in love with Elizabeth, who was travelling on the same ship en route to Mauritius where she was to be based. George could not believe his luck when he was told on arrival in Madagascar that his posting had now been changed to Mauritius. Thinking that this must be some sort of 'wind up' as everyone knew of the shipboard romance, he nearly missed boarding the ship. Coincidentally, Elizabeth and her elder sister, Janet, were born in the same street as my mother had lived in as a child in Highgate, although they had never previously met. In later years, Janet, who lived in Exeter, loved to reminisce how she had seen my mother as a baby being pushed past their house in her pram.

Elizabeth confided to us that she was soon expecting a child. I found this news rather exciting and insisted that if she gave birth to a girl she must be named Rosie after my precious rag doll. This was not to be, as Juliet Frances Ramsay was born on 7 August 1946. I was disappointed that Juliet had not been named Rosie, but very happy to have a cousin, especially a girl. They continued to live on the family farm, Kiltannon, where George now employed a manager.

An extremely unpleasant aspect for children growing up in Africa were the jiggers. They are eight legged insects that burrow into ones feet to lay their eggs, and this is incredibly itchy. For some reason, probably because I never wore shoes, I got an awful lot of them. The only people who were able to remove them were the African servants who gently probed the skin until finally with a big grin, proudly produced the jigger complete with the sac of eggs at the end of the needle. Ticks were another problem, as apart from the possibility of inflicting us with the dreaded tick bite fever, I constantly found them clinging to different parts of my body. The only way to dispose of them was to gently pull them off, but as they usually managed to remain unseen for a few days, feeding on our blood, they were so fat that when removed the blood spurted everywhere.

The health service in Kenya was rather dodgy, and I, like many other children, had my tonsils chopped off rather than having them completely removed, which of course meant that they kept growing back and had to be hacked off again. I hated this procedure as it took place on a table in the surgery with the doctor talking kindly to me, before unexpectedly smothering my face with a wad of lint seeped in ghastly smelling chloroform. After the second operation, I was determined never to repeat this horrible experience and on arriving at the surgery for my third tonsil chopping-off procedure, I ran away. My mother, with the doctor still holding the chloroform pad, frantically chased me all around Nairobi before eventually catching me, kicking and screaming, and slapping the pad over my face.

When I was seven years old, I inherited a doll which had originally belonged to Gagee when she was a child. This doll had a lovely china face, real hair and was fully dressed in her original clothes right down to her leather shoes. She also came with a small leather suitcase containing winter coats, dresses and laced up leather boots. I will never forget my excitement on receiving this precious and longed for gift, or the horror at finding her two days later after the last small guest had left my birthday party, still propped up on the chair where she had previously been placed, but with her beautiful face smashed to bits.

Although I was blessed with a charmed life with parents and grandparents who adored me as much as I did them, it was darkened by a succession of nannies who unbeknown to my parents were sometimes rather cruel. The first nanny I recall, when I was about three or four years old, was a fat Seychelloise lady (there were a lot of people from the Seychelles living in Kenya then). She enjoyed frightening me after I had gone to bed and the light had been switched off by making weird, shadowy silhouettes appear on the wall. The second one was red haired and Irish, who at the slightest provocation dragged me screaming through the house banging my head hard on every doorknob – there were a lot of doors in that house. I was petrified of her, and very relieved when she was eventually sacked after being found drunk on her bed when she was supposed to have been looking after us.

My third and fourth birthday parties – both held at Muthaiga

My third and fourth birthday parties – both held at Muthaiga

My father with my brother, Kevin, and me, Nairobi, 1945

My grandfather with my brother, Kevin, Nairobi, 1946

My mother, Pam, Kevin and me, with cousins, Elaine and Juliet, 1946

CHAPTER THREE

'GOING HOME'

Every four years we took a long holiday in England, usually sailing on a Union Castle or B.I. liner. This longed-for holiday was referred to as 'going home' which made no sense to me, as the only home I had ever known was Kenya. The first time I remember travelling to England was in 1948 when we sailed on a B.I. ship, *The Mantola*, arriving in Southampton on 15 February.

There was a great flurry of excitement as last-minute preparations were made for the voyage and holiday. My mother and I spent many hours with different Indian tailors in Nairobi, being measured up and fitted for all the warm clothes needed for an English winter. My dresses were made from viyella which my mother smocked in the evenings. Liberty bodices, vests, stockings and woollen gloves were ordered from Harrods or Swan and Edgar in Piccadilly Circus, arriving by post in plenty of time to pack. All these clothes, especially liberty bodices, seemed very strange to me, as I was used to running around in a cotton dress and whenever possible without shoes. Our clothes were packed in huge, heavy trunks with hanging spaces and drawers. Before we left, we visited the bustling, colorful market in Nairobi where we chose beautifully hand carved wooden animals to take as gifts for my parents' many friends and family in England. One event we all dreaded was the compulsory smallpox vaccinations needed for travelling abroad. These were given with a two-pronged needle which was dipped into the vaccine solution before being pricked, or more often jabbed, several times into our skin. As this vaccination left a rather unattractive mark it was usually given on the top of the thigh – if you were lucky enough to have a thoughtful doctor.

'A suitable young girl', usually someone who wanted to return to England but couldn't afford the fare, was employed as a nanny to look after my brother and me on board ship. Finally the trunks were strapped down, ready to be loaded onto the train taking us from Nairobi to Mombasa. There were masses of smiling friends waiting at Nairobi station with chocolates and cards wishing us bon voyage and copious glasses of champagne were consumed on the platform, with my parents leaping onto the train at the very last moment. I loved this train journey, happy to sit for hours with my face pressed against the window with the comforting clickety-clack of the wheels below, as the train chugged through the miles of flat, dry plains dotted with thorn bushes. I enjoyed watching the herds of zebra, giraffe and little 'Tommies' with constantly wagging tails, but my one desire was to spot a lion snoozing near a thorn bush, which I never did.

At seven o'clock a waiter wound his way up and down the train playing a crude, wooden, African styled xylophone indicating that it was time for the first sitting for dinner. We usually ate at the second sitting, as my parents liked to relax with their whisky and soda in the compartment while watching the sun setting over the plains. Dinner was served in the dining carriages, the tables set with white cloths, heavy white china and silver cutlery – all marked E.A.R. & H (East African Railways and Harbours). There was plenty of friendly laughter as the smiling African waiters tried to serve the meal on the rocky train without spilling food all over us. The waiters were often untrained and on one occasion the coffee was served before the soup, but nobody really cared as incidents like that were all part of the charm and fun of this train. On returning to our compartment we found that the backs of our seats had been lifted up on hinges to form bunks, one on top of the other, with crisp white sheets and blankets. The wooden shutters had been pulled down and the lights switched on, so that it was all comforting and snug. It was almost impossible to sleep as the train picked up speed during the night and appeared at times to be travelling dangerously fast, stopping constantly at every tiny station along the track in the middle of nowhere. There were always masses of dark eyed, almost naked, loudly chattering *totos*, who never seemed to sleep, waiting excitedly on the platform at every stop, while men crouched by the doors of their mud houses drinking and talking by the light of their kerosene lamps.

As morning broke, the air became muggy and hot and the view changed completely. Instead of thorn trees and plains there were views of tall coconut palms and baobab trees, interspersed with mud huts and more waving *totos*. As the train approached Mombasa, enticing glimpses of the sea could be seen through the palm fronds. On arriving at the station, having eventually located our luggage, we took a taxi to the harbour where our ship was waiting. A band played patriotic tunes on the quay as everybody excitedly settled into their cabins, while porters scurried around delivering chocolates, flowers and telegrams for departing passengers. When the gangplank was raised everyone on board assembled on the deck, throwing long coloured streamers while waving excitedly to the crowds below, as the ship sailed away to the sound of the band fading into the distance. The ships were extremely luxurious with parties, dancing and banquets every night. I remember feeling proud of my good-looking parents who were very sociable and seemed to spend the whole voyage eating and dancing in wonderful clothes.

The first port we stopped at was Aden, where it was extremely hot and not many passengers bothered to disembark. The ship then sailed onwards to Suez where it stopped for a short time in order to off-load cargo. Everybody loved the slow eight-hour sail through the Suez Canal where it was almost possible to touch the camels meandering in the desert on either side of the ship. The passengers were fascinated by the tall, dark Sudanese dock-workers who had the ability to stand on one leg at a time for hours on end. Due to their mass of thick, curly, black hair, my parents and their friends rudely referred to them as 'Fuzzy Wuzzies'. Our next port of call was Port Said, where the Egyptian *Gulli Gulli* men (conjurers) were hoisted on board in large wicker baskets to entertain the passengers by performing disappearing tricks with baby chickens, while naked young boys dived for pennies thrown over the ship by passengers. Other strange and interesting characters also appeared on deck, transforming the civilized and elegant atmosphere of the ship into an exciting and exotic street market selling brightly coloured leather stools and rugs. My parents usually went ashore to take tea at the famous Casino Hotel and shop at Simon Artz, a wonderful department store selling every imaginable item and staying open night and day every time a passenger ship docked. We remained on board the ship enjoying the fun with our nanny.

The buffet tables were beautifully decorated with ice sculptures and laden with exotic dishes at every meal, while smartly dressed waiters attended to the diners' every need. As we sailed into colder seas, hot mugs of beef tea were served mid-morning as the passengers relaxed on their deck chairs, their legs covered with Tartan rugs. In the afternoon deck games were organized and in the evening the passengers enjoyed playing bingo, which the rather snobbish colonialists preferred to call 'Housie Housie'. Most passengers disliked sailing through the Bay of Biscay when the ship lurched and pitched as the waves battered her sides and furniture slid in every direction. Some people were very sea sick, I certainly was, and stayed in their cabins leaving the restaurant and decks to the stalwart few.

A replacement nanny was always waiting for us at the docks in Southampton. On this occasion the new nanny was an older Scottish lady, Miss Dickie. She instantly took a dislike to me as much as I eventually began to dislike and fear her. She used every opportunity to punish me by putting me 'on silence', which meant that I was not allowed to utter a word for hours on end. She adored my brother, spending much of the time kissing and cuddling him while I cowered in a corner with a book. The minute either of my parents entered the room, she started laughing and smiling with me as if we were the greatest of friends.

★

We started our holiday in London, staying at a hotel in Belsize Park, Chatley Court Hotel, where we took two suites, one for my parents and one for my brother, myself and our nanny, Miss Dickie. My parents loved London, normally staying there for several weeks. My father spent many hours at Boodle's, a gentlemen's club in St. James's – I suppose he felt at home in clubs as he spent so much time enjoying them in Kenya. He also spent evenings gambling at the Clermont Club in London. I always felt this was totally out of character and never discovered whether he was lucky or not, as this was a subject that was not discussed. While my father relaxed in his clubs, my mother met friends for tea at Fortnum and Mason or Lyons Corner House in the Strand. She often took me with her to the tea dances at the latter, which I loved. I will never forget the elegantly dressed men and women, the opulence of the interior and the delicious walnut cake they served there. The waitresses wore black dresses with little frilly white aprons, while the orchestra played popular music discreetly in a corner as couples danced. Unfortunately they are now part of a bygone era.

It was always a treat when we stayed with my mother's relations in Yorkshire. Aunt Mary constantly produced the most wonderful meals and cakes from her Aga, which was a novelty to us as there were no Agas in Kenya. We also stayed with my mother's best friend, my godmother, Peggy, and her family who lived in a farmhouse deep in the Kent countryside. They seemed to be under the impression that because we lived in Africa we were very poor and insisted that we leave laden with their unwanted clothes, which so infuriated my father that he would, embarrassingly, dump them in the nearest field. I felt that he should have waited until we had driven a bit further away as they were bound to find them.

My parents usually took a long tour of the continent with friends, and on this occasion we were sent to what was described to us as a 'children's hotel' situated in Farnham, Surrey, with our nanny, Miss Dickie, in tow. At first I was extremely homesick as I felt as if we had been deserted. It seemed as if we stayed at this 'hotel' for months, which we probably did as my mother became ill delaying our return to Kenya. When we first arrived, the other children treated us with great suspicion as none of them had a nanny to look after them. However, Miss Dickie made lots of friends in the area and thankfully, soon forgot about her dislike of me, in fact I think she also forgot that she was being paid to look after us at all. Apart from missing my family, I was happy in Farnham. I particularly enjoyed playing freely in the woods and fields with the other children, before returning to the smell of home cooking in the evening.

While in England, my father took the opportunity of buying a new car which was shipped back to Kenya, arriving some weeks after we had returned. There was always much excitement as we waited in anticipation for the car to arrive at the docks in Mombasa where we usually picked it up. His favourite acquisition was a Humber Super Snipe – he loved that car.

★

On one of our voyages, back to Kenya in 1952 on the Union Castle ship, the *Dunnottar Castle*, the famous writer, Ernest Hemingway, was a fellow passenger. He was travelling there with his fourth wife, Mary Welsh, intending to join a safari hunting and shooting elephant. This did not impress me, as I have a great respect for all wild animals and do not believe in shooting them unnecessarily. However, his presence on board caused great excitement among the other passengers, as apart from having a magnetic personality, he was a wonderful raconteur with a wealth of stories to tell. His attractive blonde wife never socialized, but spent the entire voyage typing his latest book in the ship's library. I spent the last few days on board daring myself to ask Ernest Hemingway to sign my autograph book, which I had bought in the ship's shop especially. I eventually managed to succeed, although this was extremely difficult as the timing had to be exact. He was grumpy when he first appeared on deck, after he first started drinking he was in a good mood for a few hours, but by the afternoon he was not so affable and probably too drunk to write his signature.

Meanwhile, my wonderful, stoical grandmother, Alice, died of pneumonia at the Nairobi Hospital on 9 August 1950. She was a difficult patient while in hospital refusing to stay in bed, thus catching a chill which sadly led to her death. It was decided that our family would now live in my grandparents' house in Muthaiga, with Grandpa moving into a newly built extension at the side of the house. We just left our lovely home in Nairobi, renting it out fully furnished and moved into the house in Muthaiga with all its furniture in situ. Gagee remained in her beloved home in Nairobi. As we already had our own trusted staff some of my grandparents' servants went to live with my father's brother, George, and his family at the farm in Kiambu. Our life carried on in the same orderly manner, but with my father now playing competitive tennis and squash at the Muthaiga Club instead of the Nairobi Club, and my mother entertaining her admirers in the afternoon on a different veranda.

After Granny's death, Grandpa rapidly deteriorated. He became a recluse, never leaving his room or seeing any of his old friends. He was happy being cared for by his devoted African nurses who were ceaselessly patient and understanding with him, although he was usually extremely rude to them. Many historians and writers were eager to interview my grandfather and to write about his early years in Kenya, but although he had so much to tell, he refused to talk to any of them.

Life was good for the settlers and their families then, and none of us imagined that frightening and dangerous times lay just ahead, or that our happy, secure lives were about to change forever.

*Tea party at Muthaiga – my grandfather and my mother sitting opposite each
other next to the table, 1951*

House at Muthaiga, 1952

CHAPTER FOUR

THE MAU MAU REBELLION

In 1952, after we returned from one of our long holidays in England, there were whisperings of a terrifying movement called the Mau Mau, which had been started by a small group of particularly militant revolutionaries from the KAU (Kenyan African Union). Their main aim was to recruit as many Kikuyu as possible to join the cause, which was to attempt to drive all the white people out of Kenya, by force if necessary, thereby gaining independence. They were rebelling against British rule and the white settlers who had taken the land which they believed belonged to them. Today they would be known as freedom fighters, although that is not how I remember them, but I suppose, looking back, they thought violence was the only way they could gain their independence.

For many years discontent among the different tribes, especially the Kikuyu, had slowly been festering. The unrest intensified in 1932 after the hearing of the Morris Carter Land Commission, when it was decided to continue to maintain the White Highlands Policy restricting the Kikuyu to overcrowded reserves. Jomo Kenyatta, a well-educated Kikuyu politician, was the founder leader of the KAU who had fought for independence for many years behind the scenes. He was determined to achieve their political goal, peacefully and without violence.

The Kikuyu have always been influenced by witchcraft and superstition. They regard Mount Kenya, or *Kirinyaga*, as the sacred realm of *Ngai* (God). Their ancient Kikuyu superstitions, oaths and ceremonies, after being grossly distorted by the Mau Mau chiefs, laid the foundations for the gruesome oaths used in their initiation ceremonies. New recruits were forced to take these oaths promising to fight or die when they swore allegiance to the cause, as like most terrorist groups the Mau Mau enforced discipline by declaring that anyone who was not with them was against them. The leaders stopped at nothing to incite the Kikuyu, most of whom were very happy working for their white families, and were often prepared to die or lose their jobs rather than harm their employers. Some Kikuyu were willing to convert to the cause, but most had to be forced to take the oaths. If they resisted, as hundreds did, they and their families were dragged screaming from their huts in the middle of the night and brutally murdered. There were seven oaths, all far too gruesome to even mention here, especially the one which promised to bring the head of a white person to their leaders.

Although Jomo Kenyatta did not advocate this violence, he was nevertheless arrested and sent to prison in October 1952, where he remained for nine years. The Mau Mau became even more dangerous after his arrest, and when this news was made public they left a threatening message on a note pinned to the body of a strangled cat that had been hung on a branch of a tree in Kiambu. This chillingly read: "We are going to Mount Kenya but will return like lightning." Kenya was now in the grip of terror as the Mau Mau, literally, initiated a war against the British Colonial Government from the forest. Thousands of terrorists fled to the beautiful equatorial Aberdare forest, where many of them stayed in hiding, often with their families, for several years. They became wild and savage, their hair grew long, matted and lice ridden, and they wore nothing but animal skins. They never starved, as they ventured down from the forest in gangs at night, carrying pangas and knives in order to steal cattle from farms to eat or to sacrifice for one of their rituals. Not content with this, they often cruelly mutilated the animals leaving farmers to find them in the morning half dead with their legs hacked off.

★

The majority of the Mau Mau did not live in the Aberdare Forest, but in, and around Nairobi, or on remote farms, often working among us as servants in our homes. This naturally created a great deal of mistrust, mostly unjustified, but many people were wary of employing a Kikuyu as they never knew whether oaths had been taken or not. My mother who had just employed a Kikuyu chauffeur decided that it would be safer to drive herself around Nairobi until everything settled down, and reluctantly asked him to leave. Many of the new recruits to the Mau Mau were bravely loyal to their employers, despite the fact that they had probably been forced to join the rebellion against their will and take at least two of the oaths.

Mau Mau gangs soon began attacking white families' homes, especially isolated farms, usually sneaking stealthily into the house with their pangas or simis after darkness had fallen. They normally entered through the back door leading to the kitchen while the family were eating their dinner, with or without the help of the servants, and hacking the occupants to death. We read about these horrific killings in the *East African Standard* often of people known to us, such as the case of a little boy who had been innocently riding his bicycle near his home when a small gang captured him – and horrors of horrors, decapitated him. Another of my parents' friends was taken from his house by about sixty terrorists and buried alive facing Mount Kenya, after his wife had been savagely murdered in front of him.

One of the first, and most brutal murders occurred when a gang attacked a white family, the Rucks, who lived on an isolated farm in the Kinangop, about twenty miles from Naivasha. One Saturday night, just after the young couple had tucked their six year old son up in bed and were relaxing in the sitting room before dinner, their houseboy appeared at the door with the news that there were some farm workers at the kitchen door who were concerned about a sick horse. Roger Ruck went outside to investigate, but was instantly grabbed by a small Mau Mau gang who gagged him and held him prisoner until his pregnant wife, Esme, a doctor, came to look for him. He was then brutally murdered in front of her, before she and her unborn baby were hacked to death. The gang then went upstairs where a faithful Kikuyu servant had locked their terrified little boy, Michael, in the bedroom and horribly killed both of them, leaving the room scattered with blood covered toys. Apparently some of the murderers were trusted farm workers who had recently joined the Mau Mau.

After reading about this particular tragedy in the *East African Standard*, I felt very nervous at night, especially as we had a forest, the Karura Forest, at the bottom of our garden where there had been some minor incidents. A couple of our friends in Muthaiga had been attacked by the Mau Mau, but luckily survived. Most of our servants were from the Luo tribe, but our neighbours employed Kikuyu staff, and one morning their cook was found hanging from a tree, having chosen to take his own life rather than follow through his promise to take the head of a white man, probably his employer, to his elders. My parents, like most people in Kenya, kept a revolver constantly at their side, although I doubt my mother would have known how to use it if the occasion ever arose. My father joined the Home Guard, taking his turn with the neighbours to safeguard our homes at night, armed with his revolver and a torch, patrolling his patch until the early hours. His absence left us even more vulnerable, as not only were we without a man in the house, but also without any form of protection apart from our police whistles. We each kept one of these whistles by our bed, putting our blind trust in them, but knowing deep down that no one would have dared to come to our aid had we blown them.

★

On 21 October the British Colonial Government declared a 'state of emergency' and many children were sent to England to live with friends and family, but our parents, thankfully, did not consider this option. My parents kept their bedroom door locked at night to avoid the possibility of us wandering into the room, being mistaken for an intruder, and being shot. I was told that if I heard anyone creeping up the stairs during the night, I was to rush to my wardrobe, which had sliding doors running along the width of the wall, and hide in a small cupboard behind my clothes. This tiny closet with a door and a bolt had been especially constructed into the eaves for this purpose. My parents and brother had similar hiding places in their bedrooms, therefore, in the event of a Mau Mau attack we would all be hiding in terror in separate places. Fortunately, we never had to put this frightening plan into action. Nevertheless, I lay awake for hours every night, frozen with fear, my imagination running riot as every floorboard in the large old house creaked.

One night we woke to the sound of blood curdling screams coming from the house below us. We realized that the family who lived there were being attacked, but there was nothing we could do except frantically blow our police whistles. It was hopeless trying to phone the police, as they never came. We liked to think that the noise made from our whistles helped to chase the gang away as the family were fortunately unhurt. It also helped that they had erected a steel gate across the top of the stairs – we called them 'rape gates', which in this case proved strong enough to keep the terrorists out.

Although it was a terrifying time for white families because the rebellion was aimed at us, in the end only about thirty-two white people were murdered. The real victims were the thousands of innocent Kikuyu who just wanted a peaceful route to independence, but because of this were horribly and unnecessarily killed. The worst atrocity occurred on 26 March 1953 in Limuru (where I was at boarding school) when a Mau Mau gang butchered, disemboweled and burnt about 120 innocent Kikuyu women and children whose husbands had refused to join the uprising. Some Kikuyu women had also joined the rebellion, and this particular attack was led by one of them.

The families' huts were set alight as they slept, after being barricaded up by the terrorists so that they could not escape. This became known as the 'Lari Massacre' or 'The Night of the Long Knives', which finally helped to bring this appalling uprising to the attention of the world. I will never forget watching in horror from our dormitory windows on that terrible evening, as the flames spectacularly lit up the sky as they devoured the whole village.

Eventually, the British Government started fighting back and four battalions were brought over from England, including the Black Watch and the Lancashire Fusiliers. A few exceptionally brave white volunteers from the Special Forces of the Kenya Regiment, who had been born in Kenya, agreed to disguise themselves as Mau Mau, take their barbaric oaths and live with the gangs in the Aberdare Forest. We called them 'pseudo gangs'. They dressed in dirty rags, grew and dyed their hair black, painted their bodies with potassium permanganate and put a blob of boot polish inside their eyes to turn the whites into the yellowish colour of the Kikuyu man's eyes. One of the main aims of the 'pseudo gangs' was to hunt down and catch the dangerous leaders such as 'General' Dedan Kimathi who was one of the most treacherous and dreaded of the Mau Mau leaders. He had lived in the forest since the beginning of the rebellion and become like a wily animal that was almost impossible to locate. To our relief, he was eventually captured, tried, and hanged in 1956, which helped to bring this dark chapter in the history of Kenya to an end. Intriguingly, the day he was hanged was the day the large tree he used to worship under in the Aberdare forest, sensationally, crashed to the ground.

It must not be forgotten, and has subsequently been brought to light that the British troops had perpetrated equally evil deeds on thousands of innocent Kikuyu and Luo people, as well as known Mau Mau and suspected Mau Mau. Thankfully these violent times are now long gone and closure for the surviving Mau Mau complainants was achieved when the British courts awarded them millions of pounds in compensation for these past atrocities.

CHAPTER FIVE

LIMURU GIRLS' SCHOOL AND LATER

In September 1952, I started my first term at Limuru Girls' School, a Church of England boarding school, which had been established by Arnold Butler McDonnell in 1923 and was run by Mary Roseveare and Margaret Lister. Arnold McDonnell dreamed up the idea of starting a girls' school, as he could not find a suitable local school for his four daughters. Limuru (or Rongai, as it is known by the Africans) climbs almost 3,000 feet. Although this only covers a distance of twelve miles from Muthaiga, it feels like travelling into an unknown, cool and verdant world.

Trying to look sporty at Limuru Girls' School – me, standing, in the middle

We all wore brown blazers, brown cardigans, brown dresses, sturdy brown shoes, socks and braided sashes around our waists, but at the weekends we changed into white socks and coloured dresses, the colour depending on which House we belonged to. I was in Lister, and therefore wore a yellow dress. The sashes were also brown, but it was possible to earn a red sash for good deportment and a green one for excellent deportment. It was my dream to exchange my brown sash for at least a red one, but despite walking up and down the dormitory for hours with books on my head, to my dismay, I never achieved this goal.

The school was set in beautiful lush, green grounds, with a sweeping driveway which at certain times of the year was carpeted with indescribably beautiful blue flowers which had fallen from the jacaranda trees on either side of the drive. We were all very proud of the recently completed chapel, which stood between the main building and the various *bandas* (wooden huts) which were used as classrooms. On looking back, our dormitories were rather like large prison cells as we slept on iron bedsteads with hard lumpy mattresses and thin blankets – it was freezing at night in Limuru. We dreaded the sound of the rising bell each cold morning when we were jerked back into reality from a deep sleep, brought on, we all thought, by overwork!

I hated the lack of privacy, as I am a person who has to have my own space and here there was no chance. I discovered that I was considered by the teachers and my peers to be rebellious and naughty and was always getting into trouble of some kind, mainly for talking in the corridor, which was a huge sin. Once my punishment was to attempt to cut right round the edges of the hockey pitch with nail scissors, and another time to stand on a stool and sing nursery rhymes to the prefects. The meals were revolting, typical boarding school food, but we were forced to eat it. I recall once being served a pig's heart dumped in the middle of the plate. I refused to eat it and sat in the dining room on my own for hours as the heart became colder and colder. However, much as I disliked this school, and the food, some wonderful life long friends were made there and for that I am very grateful.

The school employed a strange assortment of teachers, and I don't think we learnt very much while there, certainly, I didn't. Mrs Hayes was our much respected and beloved science teacher, despite making us blow up rabbits' bladders covered in blood, and dissect white mice which had been kept in cages and then killed especially for this purpose – I can't think how this was meant to help us in later life. Miss Ford or Fordie, as we called her, was our rather plump, unpopular, whiskery faced geography teacher and Twiga (Swahili for giraffe) named because she was so tiny was our very popular history teacher.

We were fortunate to have had a wonderful headmistress, Miss Anne Fisher, who ran the school efficiently with a kind, but firm hand. On Sunday evenings everyone looked forward to assembling in the junior common room for what was strangely called 'silent reading', when Miss Fisher would read us popular, well written books in her lovely melodious voice. She was highly religious, which was not surprising as her uncle was Geoffrey Fisher, the then Archbishop of Canterbury. We were thrilled when he visited Kenya and our School in 1955, and felt very honoured and special when after giving the service in the school chapel, he blessed every single one of us. After his visit, some of us, including myself, became born again Christians and spent many hours reading the bible, discussing theology, collecting Holy pictures and trying to be good!

Matron, a rather stern-looking grey-haired lady, also had a claim to fame as she nursed Queen Mary in her last months, before coming to live in Kenya.

Miss Fisher, headmistress of Limuru Girls' School, with the Archbishop of Canterbury outside the school chapel

The only time we ever left the confines of the school during the term, apart from half term or the odd day out, was when we were transported in an open cattle truck, seated opposite each other on wooden benches, to netball or hockey matches played against other schools. If we had successfully beaten our opponents at whatever sport we were playing, we returned singing the school anthem, *In Fide Vade* – which I think means 'Walk in Faith' – at the top of our voices so that the rest of the girls knew we were returning victorious. If we had lost the match we sang *'We'll be coming down the mountain when we come.'*

Most of the girls lived on farms and as they belonged to the Young Farmers' Club, some weekends were spent at various rallies or helping at Uplands Pig Farm, where they produced wonderful pork pies. The rest of us, dressed in our colourful weekend dresses, enjoyed playing popular records under the shade of the jacaranda trees on a wind-up gramophone.

★

During the Mau Mau emergency the school was surrounded by barbed wire, with four or five high 'look out' posts manned by fine young men from the 'Devons' (The Devonshire and Dorset regiment) and 'Buffs' (Royal East Kent regiment) – British regiments who had been sent to Kenya to try and quell the rebellion. These guards lived for a time in the junior common room and were on duty day and night ready to fight in the event of an attack by the Mau Mau. They were the only males we ever saw during the term, and we were all very happy to have these tough, good-looking young men protecting us. An older, rather portly man, Gibson, was in charge of security and lived with his wife in a small cottage to the right of the school. We took it in turns to arrange the flowers in their home for fifty cents a time, and enjoyed counting the numerous empty gin bottles hidden under his bed!

'Operation Hockey Sticks' would have to come into play if the Mau Mau ever managed to climb through the barbed wire and past the armed guards. We all kept our hockey sticks under our beds, prepared to fight the intruders with them, if necessary, to the bitter end. We had one attempted Mau Mau attack, which happened to coincide with an incident when three other girls and myself had wandered to the edge of the boundaries of the protected school grounds to smoke cigarettes, which of course was strictly forbidden. We were thoroughly enjoying our freedom, and the cigarettes, when dozens of crazed looking natives with long matted hair and wild eyes poured down the hill from the forest behind, sharp pangas swinging ominously from their hands. Terrified though we were by this sight, when a battered old Land Rover screamed up to rescue us, we were far more concerned about being caught smoking than the prospect of being murdered! The guards unceremoniously and speedily bundled us into the Land Rover and drove us at hair-raising speed back to the school, where we grabbed our hockey sticks and dived under our beds. The older girls were already lined up on the stairs prepared to blind the Mau Mau with pepper from the school pepper pots, while the school bell rang out loudly. Fortunately, this particular Mau Mau gang was frightened back to the forest by our guards before they could enter the double doors of the school, but not before a couple of the bandits had been shot and killed in the conflict.

Smoking at Limuru Girls' School, me in the middle

I dreaded the drive from our home in Muthaiga to Limuru, as although we passed flourishing banana groves, green fields and friendly Kikuyu women, bent double as they carried firewood on their backs, the leather straps biting into their foreheads, it was a dangerous road. There was a Mau Mau settlement, Banana Hill, situated about half way to Limuru, which consisted of hundreds of round mud huts built in terraces up the hillside, with the smoke from the pungent smell of their cooking fires drifting down the hill – there were rumours that the radical young Mau Mau leaders had their headquarters there. We always kept our car windows shut on this drive to avoid the stones that were being thrown at us by the hostile men standing at the side of the road, but our main concern was that we would be lucky enough to avoid being met by the sight of large stones laid across the road forcing us to stop.

Occasionally my parents arrived at the school with my brother, Kevin, to take me and a friend to tea at the nearby Brackenhurst Hotel, an attractive Tudor-style building with dark beams crisscrossed on a white-washed exterior, set in green fields. This hotel and the surroundings were so typically English that it looked as if it belonged in a village in Surrey, rather than in the middle of Africa. An open fire warmed the rooms, which were adorned with copper pots, and the waiters wheeled in trolleys laden with an assortment of sandwiches, scones and cakes. I didn't see much of Kevin as he was boarding at Pembroke House in Gilgil and our holidays didn't coincide. He later started at Millfield School in Somerset, before attending The Royal Agricultural College in Cirencester.

★

There was great excitement when Princess Elizabeth and Prince Philip visited Kenya in early 1952 en route to Australia. Schoolchildren excitedly lined the streets of Nairobi waving flags, and my parents were among the lucky residents who were presented to them at a garden party held at Government House. The Kenya Government presented the Royal couple with a specially built and locally furnished timber house, Sagana Lodge, situated in a remote area on the slopes of Mount Kenya. It was while they were staying there, having first visited Treetops for a few nights, that George VI died on 6 February 1952, and Princess Elizabeth became Queen Elizabeth II.

The Mau Mau did not deter most people from continuing to stay in remote camps or game lodges, and one of our favorite places was Treetops. This small basic wooden hotel was set high in the branches of a large wild fig tree overlooking a salt lick water hole in the forest, about 15 miles from Nyeri, at the foot of the Aberdares.

Princess Elizabeth at the garden party at Government House, Nairobi 1952

The bouquet presented by 'Prince' bin Salim' the son of a coastal Swahili boy called 'Prince' after Prince Charles, who was the same age.

THE QUEEN'S MESSAGE
TO THE GOVERNOR AND
PEOPLE OF KENYA

"**O**N RETURNING TO ENGLAND MY HUSBAND AND I SEND OUR warmest thanks to you and to the people of Kenya for the wonderful welcome you gave us during our visit.

" Although the tragic death of my father prevented us from seeing Mombasa, it was a great pleasure to meet so many subjects of the late King whom I am now proud to call my own.

" Among our many experiences we particularly enjoyed the happy and restful days at the Lodge, which surpassed our keenest expectations, and to which we greatly hope to return.

" We hope that you will convey our sincere appreciation and thanks to all who combined in the admirable arrangements which were made for our reception."

Letter written to the people of Kenya by the Queen after her 1952 trip to Kenya.

Treetops, 1955

On our frequent visits to Treetops, we stopped for lunch in Nyeri at a low grey-stone, red-roofed hotel, surrounded by colourful flower beds and set in beautiful grounds, The Outspan, before climbing into a Land Rover and being driven to the edge of the forest. On our arrival, we disembarked following the armed guard through the game infested forest with only the sound of crackling leaves beneath our feet, as we walked the mile and a half to our hotel in the tree. The forest was teeming with wild animals in those days and it really was necessary to have an armed guard, whereas today this would probably be 'staged' to impress the tourists.

On arriving safely at the hotel, we climbed a steep 35" wooden ladder onto a wide veranda where tea and cake was served while we were observed by a troupe of playful baboons. They eventually picked up courage to greedily snatch the cake from our plates and run back into the trees to enjoy their loot. Our eyes, however, were constantly fixed on the waterhole where an assortment of bushbuck, giant forest pigs, exotic birds and occasionally buffalo or elephant appeared. Dinner was served in the small, wooden dining room at one long candlelit table which seated twenty-two guests.

Everyone spoke in whispers so as not to disturb the animals while we tucked into a meal consisting of asparagus, fried fish, chicken pie with vegetables and pêche flambée with cream, followed by coffee and brandy on the veranda. On retiring to our bedrooms we found a paraffin lamp by the door, hot water bottles in our beds and our clothes hanging up on the branches of the tree, which protruded through the floor and into the small wooden rooms. Of course everybody wanted to see elephant, rhino, and best of all, leopard. If any of these animals came to drink at the waterhole during the night or very early in the morning, we were woken up by a discreet knock on the door and an excited whispered *"upesi, upesi, iku tembo"* – "hurry, hurry there are elephants." Some guest remained on the veranda all night, wrapped up warmly, in aircraft chairs which had been donated by a friendly aircraft company. Soon after our last visit in 1953, Treetops was burnt to the ground by the Mau Mau. A much larger, more sophisticated hotel was built in its stead, but the intimacy of the original small hotel in the tree was, sadly, never replaced.

★

An even more magical retreat for us was the far more basic tiny camp in Amboseli, situated on a dry soda lake on Kenya's southern border with

Tanganiyka (now Tanzania). It consisted of six simple tents in the middle of scrubland with Mount Kilimanjaro towering majestically above. Each tent had two camp beds, a table, paraffin lamps and chopped wood for a fire, not only to cook our meals on but also to keep the animals at bay. The 'long drop' was, as usual, situated some distance from our tents, consequently, it helped to have a strong bladder, especially at night. There were no guards or game rangers here, usually just the animals, the birds, the heat, the dust and us. There can be no experience as wonderful as watching the sun set while sitting in the middle of Africa, with no other sound but the African night birds and the roars, grunts and calls of the animals as they go about their nightly pursuits. Usually from the comfort of our camp chairs we enjoyed watching Gertie, the resident rhino, with her four-foot horn, later broken off in a fight, elegant giraffes, sometimes with their babies, delicately munching from nearby acacia trees, hundreds of shiny blue starlings darting from bush to bush and the friendly, playful rock hyrax. Once a pride of loose-limbed lions padded past us almost within our touching distance, as we held our breath, but they seemed unaware of our existence and walked onwards into the distance.

Often at dawn, we were lucky enough to be treated to the sight of a herd of elephant suddenly materializing from the nearby trees, treading quietly in a line, babies in tow, past our tent. Before leaving the camp we tucked into a hearty breakfast, which we had cooked on the open fire, while watching the clouds magically break to reveal the magnificent snow-capped mountain top. After breakfast we unfailingly studied the paw prints to discover how close the animals had been prowling to our tents the night before. It was probably just as well that we were not aware at the time just how near they had actually been.

During the rains the powdery white surface of Amboseli's dry soda lake often flooded, turning it into a shallow basin, attracting large herds of every species of animal and bird. The allure of seeing so many wild animals was tempting, but, unfortunately, during this time it was impossible to visit as the road was impassable.

Another popular safari was to spend a couple of nights at Ngorongoro Crater in Tanganiyka where we stayed in a welcoming lodge made of logs. We invariably arrived after a very muddy and slippery drive up the mountain road, the car's wheels skidding in the sticky black mud from the rain that had fallen the previous night. The rooms consisted of wooden bandas clinging to the very edge of the crater. It was always misty and cold in this mountainous terrain, and we were grateful for the fires burning in the main part of the lodge where guests gathered for a drink at the bar before consuming an early meal. In the morning due to the steep, treacherous descent to the crater floor, we usually swapped our car for one of the Land Rovers with chains, driven by a game warden. On one occasion, due to the lack of any game wardens available that day, the Land Rover was driven by the resident bar man who was obviously very drunk or 'high' on bhang (cannabis). It was a terrifying ride as he drove dangerously fast, skidding and sliding round the twisty bends until with relief we reached the bottom of the crater, leaving the mist and cold behind. We were now bathed in warmth and sunshine and surrounded by thousands of animals, roaming freely, protected from the dangers of the world. The Ngorongoro Crater is the largest crater in the world, an expanse of flat green land, twelve miles across, enclosed by steep mountainous walls, two thousand feet high.

★

We continued our bi-annual holidays to the coast, sometimes taking my beloved train from Nairobi to Mombasa, or travelling the three-hundred miles through desolate, dusty bush by car, stopping en route at a hotel at Mtito Andei for lunch. The pretty, rustic hotel stood alone in an oasis of greenery and flowers, with the Union Jack flying bravely at the entrance. We continued our journey until we reached the hotel at Voi, which is about half way to the coast, to spend the night and enjoy a welcome break from the dust and isolation of the road. We slept in simple bandas, undressing and reading by the light of our hurricane lamps. Before going to bed we usually washed our dust-soaked socks and hung them up on the hotel drying line, but were amazed to find in the morning that they had disappeared. We later discovered that they had been eaten during the night by an ostrich, Willie, with a very peculiar taste in food!

According to local lore, the name 'Voi' comes from a slave trader called Chief Kivoi who settled there about four-hundred years ago.

On arriving at Mombasa we usually started with a curry lunch on the shady veranda of the Manor Hotel, before taking another very hot and bumpy ride to our final destination. We enjoyed crossing Mtwapa Creek on the ferry at Shimo-la-Tewa, where the ferry men sang catchy Swahili songs as they pulled on the chains propelling the crudely made wooden craft across the creek. Our favourite hotels were Jadini Beach on the palm fringed south coast or Lawfords in Malindi, an ancient little Arab town with decaying stone houses, a small white mosque and Arab women dressed from head to foot in black, their faces heavily veiled. While staying at Lawfords my father loved to surf, catching the enormous waves just before they broke, not standing up as most people do now, but lying flat on the board. At full tide the sea came right up to the verandas of the front row of rooms – now you can't even see the sea from the newly modernized building. All the hotels in those days were fairly basic, built in the traditional Kenya style with woven *macuti* roofs supported by *bariti* poles and deep, spacious verandas. We were certain to know most of the other guests who were staying there at the same time, which was not always a good thing!

On one of our later holidays while staying at Tradewinds Hotel on the south coast, my father decided to visit the property our family owned at Port Reitz in Mombasa. This was the plot of land with its own deserted beach and small thatched dwelling my grandfather had proudly bought for his bride all those years ago. Our family had not bothered to renovate it as that particular part of Mombasa had never been developed as a holiday destination, as a result the place was pretty derelict. On this particular occasion my father was lucky to survive as he was greeted by a gang of angry African squatters screaming in Swahili, "Get off our land, or we will kill you." He shouted back at them, that it was in fact *his* land and he would get them evicted, but they turned nasty and started chasing him, angrily brandishing pangas. Luckily, he managed to leap into the car and drive off at break neck speed, eventually shaking them off. Needless to say, none of the family ever returned and the land and dwelling were sold for a pittance just before my parents left Kenya.

Another place that always pulled us back for a visit was the ruin of Gede in Malindi. It is an old Swahili town which had been lived in since the 12th century, but suddenly all the inhabitants deserted it in the 16th century. It is thought that the inhabitants were wealthy Muslims who traded with people from all over the world, as among other items, pieces of Ming vases and necklaces from Italy have been found there. It remains a mystery why the people left in such a hurry, apparently leaving food half eaten on the tables. Among the ruins are part of a palace, a mosque and some stone houses surrounded by ancient gnarled baobab trees, the trunks of which in certain lights resemble ghostly old faces. The whole place is dark, still, secretive and eerie, the only sound being the humming of insects. The local people believe the ruins are protected by the spirits of priests and that the 'old ones' will curse anyone who harms or removes anything from the site. It was said that it was impossible to take a photo of anything in Gede, and when I was young that was true, the photo never appeared, but now with modern technology it is probably different, what a shame!

My grandfather's land at Port Reitz, 1920

Me, enjoying the beach at Malindi, 1960

CHAPTER SIX

THE DEATH OF A PIONEER

My grandfather, George Ernest Ramsay, died on 18 April 1953, bedridden, but fighting to the last as he had done throughout his life. It was fitting that he should end his days in the house he had built in Muthaiga, where he and my grandmother had spent so many happy years. My grandparents are, strangely, buried in section seven, lot 67 and 68 at the City Park Cemetery in Nairobi and not in Nairobi South Cemetery where most pioneers are laid to rest – probably because it was closer to Muthaiga. It was distressing to discover on my last visit that this cemetery had been trashed with most of the stone crosses lying broken on the ground. I would have liked to visit their graves, but apparently it is now a dangerous place in which to venture.

Grandpa was an exceptional man, not only to have survived the hardships of the early days in Kenya, but also to have made his fortune from scratch by sheer hard work and guts. He was extremely generous to friends and family who were not as financially secure as he was, but remained a modest, self-effacing man. Not many people, apart from his closest friends or business associates, ever knew how successful he became. I discovered while researching his French mother's family origins that among his many acts of kindness he had paid for the funeral of a distant, unknown relation in England, Poppy Le Plastrier, who had apparently died destitute. It saddens me that it is largely unknown that the huge success of Gailey and Roberts was due to the hard work put in by my grandfather and James Gailey who were partners, and not David Roberts and James Gailey as is recorded, as David Roberts died in 1915. I feel certain that this is mainly due to the fact that the company name was never changed to Gailey and Ramsay, my grandfather's reticence and the lack of company records that exist today. The only record we found in Company House in Nairobi was the signed agreement when my grandfather became the third partner with James Gailey and his wife, Gladys in 1924, and later Chairman.

After Grandpa's death, the responsibility for looking after all the family's financial interests, such as Yasmar, Gailey and Ramsay and Kasarini Investments (James Gailey had also been my grandfather's partner in other businesses) fell onto my father's shoulders. Although diligent, he was not an entrepreneur as my grandfather had been. He found these new responsibilities a terrible burden and spent many hours locked up in his study with his ledgers spread all over the roll top desk. My father was lucky that he had never really needed to work for a living, but like his father and brother, he was a modest man and at one stage took a job as a junior civil servant rather than be seen as a gentleman of leisure.

My mother, meanwhile, became very involved with the Royal Overseas Women's League, attending their meetings once a month. She enjoyed organizing charity garden parties, held in the grounds of our house in Muthaiga, to raise money for Weal House which was being built as the first care home for the elderly in Kenya, and is happily serving this purpose today. She also gave up her time to act as an invigilator for an Indian secondary college in a rather seedy area near River Road.

To my delight, when I was fifteen, my mother decided that I needed private dancing lessons. I thoroughly enjoyed these classes, which were taken in a large empty room on the top floor of a rather dilapidated block of flats in River Road with an Indian tailor's shop, selling elaborate saris and materials in every colour, on the ground floor. My teacher was an extremely good-looking young Goan man and he and I danced the cha-cha-cha, rumba and foxtrot for nearly two hours every other day, with the music coming from a wind-up gramophone. However, this pleasurable past time was hastily stopped when some of my mother's friends pointed out that it was not a good idea for me to be alone in such an isolated, squalid place with a young attractive coloured man!

Cookery class at Winkfield Place

Winkfield Place, 1956

Although my mother was always beautifully dressed, unlike her contemporaries who imported expensive clothes from London or Paris, she preferred to buy most of her clothes from a second-hand shop, The Thrift Shop. I found this extremely embarrassing as she could certainly afford to buy as many imported clothes as she desired, and the chances of meeting one of the original owners of the outfits at a party was very likely. The clothes were of course almost new, as who would want to be seen in the same dress twice in Nairobi?

Teenage party at a house in Muthaiga (me at the back) 1956

To my horror, when I was sixteen my parents decided that I should leave Limuru Girls' School, which I was just beginning to like, and attend a finishing school to have my rough edges smoothed, Winkfield Place, known as 'Winkfield', a small manor house deep in the Berkshire countryside. This establishment was owned and run by Constance Spry, who was well known for flower arranging and had also written a comprehensive cookery book. Even worse, I learnt that I would have to fly to England on my own. I found this prospect very daunting as it was the first time I had ever been on an aircraft as our family always travelled by ship. I can remember that first BOAC flight on a *Britannia* aircraft very clearly as it took hours and hours. In those days we boarded the airplane at Nairobi's old Eastleigh airport, the former

129

Royal Air Force base, the plane bumping along the dusty runway, churning up huge billows of red earth, as it took off into the air. The plane stopped at Entebe, Khartoum, Cairo and Rome, before finally reaching London. At Khartoum there was no proper airport building, so we sat in deck chairs just off the runway, drinking bottled orange juice while waiting for the aircraft to re fuel. I was horribly sick for most of the journey, and most grateful for the sturdy brown paper bags that were tucked into the pockets at the back of the seats in front.

On arriving in London I was met by my godfather, 'Jackie' Jackson (he was stationed in Nairobi during the war and was one of my mother's staunchest admirers) and his wife Corrie. I did not really know them, but they were wonderful to me, treating me like the daughter they had never had. Corrie took me to Harrods where I was kitted out with a winter coat and other warm outfits, which in her opinion would be suitable for life at a finishing school. It was just as well that I was not given any choice in the matter as I had absolutely no idea about winter clothes, or indeed what was fashionable and what was not.

A beautiful girl, Henrietta Tiarks, who had started at Winkfield a term earlier, was chosen to look after me when I first arrived. I liked, and felt at ease with her as she had also lived abroad for a time and had no airs or graces. However, unknown to the rest of us she had already caught *the* prize – the future 14th Duke of Bedford, better known as the Marquess of Tavistock. On the whole my peers were socially oceans apart and spent most of the time discussing their rather unattractive weak chinned boy friends – referred to by us 'non debutantes' as 'Hooray Henrys' or 'Debs Delights' – the 'Kenya Cowboys' beat them hands down!

I was thrilled when a friend invited me to join their table at the Royal Military Academy Sandhurst ball. My blind date for the evening was Lord Edmund Fermoy, which sounded promising – my mother would be delighted! We all met at one of the girl's parents' houses in Ascot where her father plied us with gin and tonics. It was the most wonderful event, starting off with a very formal, but delicious dinner accompanied by copious bottles of champagne, followed by dancing to well known bands and singers playing in different marquees. I remember Joe Loss and his band was in one of them and Cliff Richard in another. The party ended in the early hours with a hearty breakfast, before we all spilled out into the streets of Camberley, mingling with the shoppers, still in our evening dresses and the men in their dinner jackets.

As Winkfield Place was a finishing school, as well as learning how to cook and arrange flowers, we were taught all the social graces of the day. Lady Isobel Barnett was responsible for showing us how to walk properly with an umbrella, extricate ourselves gracefully from the back seat of a car without showing our knickers and how to treat the butler. All this was rather unnecessary and confusing for an ordinary girl from Kenya who had never even owned an umbrella. Most of the girls who attended Winkfield were aristocrats who were about to become debutantes, and hopefully catch a Lord. There was certainly not much chance of me achieving either of these dubious goals. Much later, Lady Isobel Barnett, who was an elegant, attractive and wealthy woman, was found stealing a small item from a local shop. Unable to cope with all the adverse press, she, sadly, committed suicide.

I was not particularly happy at Winkfield as having attended a boarding school, surrounded by barbed wire, where at one time it was forbidden to receive a letter from a boy, I longed to be completely free of all restrictions. I thoroughly enjoyed the freedom at the weekends when I took trains all over the country for the first time in my life. I loved the excitement of London, especially the bohemian atmosphere and buzz of Carnaby Street. Friends of my parents invited me for weekends, but it soon dawned on me that if any of these kind people were having guests for lunch or dinner, they expected me to arrange their flowers and rustle up some wonderful meal. This I was unable to do, as I had never so much as boiled an egg at home, and hardly attended any of the flower arranging classes and as few of the cookery classes as possible – how I regret my nonchalance now! Despite my lack of interest in cooking, I left, as did all the girls, proudly clutching my Cordon Bleu certificate.

There were some perks bestowed on the pupils at Winkfield such as being invited to Henley, Royal Ascot and the polo at Windsor, where we were entertained in the Royal enclosures. We were welcomed through the famous 'red door' of Elizabeth Arden's Salon in London where she taught us how to apply our makeup and we had our hair cut by Vidal Sassoon. One of the girls I shared a room with was Lady Elizabeth Anson. She often took tea with her aunt in Windsor on Sundays and occasionally asked me to accompany her, but I always politely refused – much later I heard that the aunt she visited so regularly was the Queen Mother.

After I left Winkfield my parents were at a loss what to do with me. It was suggested that maybe I could become a fashion model and train at Lucy Clayton in London, or even worse attend another finishing school in

Switzerland. Eventually, after much persuasion on my part, it was agreed that I start a secretarial course at Temple College in Nairobi. Surprisingly, I was quite good at shorthand and typing and actually enjoyed my time there. It probably helped that I was back where I belonged, Africa.

After finishing at Temple College, I landed the job as secretary to the manager of the Christian Book Shop, which I loved. This shop was the only good book shop in Nairobi and sold novels and biographies as well as Christian books and Bibles. I borrowed my mother's yellow mini and drove from Muthaiga to my job in Government Road every day, feeling very 'grown up' and independent.

Life was good for young people in those days, especially girls, as there were still an abundance of soldiers from different regiments of the British Army in Kenya as well as the local boys, many of whom we had known since childhood. I had several different boy friends who took me to the cinema or to dances, but I didn't have a serious, steady boyfriend until I was nineteen – my parents were far too strict.

Dressed in full-skirted dresses, elastic belts and petticoats with several layers of different coloured net, friends and I would attend dances at the clubs in Kiambu, Nairobi and Parklands and the annual Kenya Regiment ball. Every New Year's Eve our family attended the ball at the Muthaiga Club, where, rather like the Happy Valley days, it became a rowdy occasion as midnight approached. After the fireworks, a huge bonfire was lit and at midnight, a young man, I think it was Francis Erskine, would climb the high burning heap of straw, slowly discarding his clothes until he reached the top, completely naked, when he would leap off just in time!

In those days we had a drive-in cinema situated on the Thika road, which was known as 'the sex pit' as courting couples could kiss or make love in the comfort of their car in darkness, while the film showed on a huge outside screen. There were also a couple of night clubs, the best one being the Equator Club which had an African décor with zebra skins and Maasai shields hanging from the walls. There was a wonderful resident African band which played until the early hours without stopping. We usually danced until the bitter end before either eating breakfast at the club or driving to Hippo Pool in the Nairobi game park. We enjoyed picnicking under the thorn trees on the banks of the pool while listening to the snorts of the hippos – they had, hopefully, all gone back into the water by then. It was so peaceful watching the pink and gold sun rise over the plains as the insects hummed around us, brilliant little, scarlet, indigo and emerald sun birds darted from tree to tree while awkward-looking secretary birds with their ragged head feathers wandered around looking confused. Later, we usually took a drive round the park hoping to see leopard and lions. Early morning or evening is the best time to spot them and at this time of day we were normally the only vehicle in the game park. We usually saw a pride of lion, and sometimes a kill, but rarely any leopard. I remember once later in the morning watching a pride of lion with some playful cubs enjoying their kill under a thorn tree, when other cars began to arrive forming a semi circle while people took photos. Suddenly, to our amazement, one of the car doors opened and a man with his camera stepped out of the car and started walking right up to the lions. Luckily for him, he was quickly stopped from being grabbed by the lioness by one of the game wardens who happened to arrive just at the right moment in his Land Rover.

A group of us teenagers loved to go to various clubs and halls where our friend, Hank, (Roger Whittacker) was singing. He was educated at The Prince of Wales boys' school where he sang in the school choir, and sometimes in the holidays was a guest singer at The Equator Club among other places, before becoming world famous. Although he was quite a bit older than us we all fancied him, but he had a long-term girl friend. Sadly, many years later his parents were murdered in Kenya.

★

Meanwhile on the Kenyan political front, after a succession of constitutional conferences at Marlborough House and Lancaster House, and after Jomo Kenyatta had been released from prison, it was agreed that Kenya was to have an interim government with a promise of universal elections one year later. The battle for eventual power and leadership was between the Kenya African Democratic Union (KADU) and the Kenya African National Union (KANU), which was led by Jomo Kenyatta. KADU were intent on having a regional system, dividing the country into administrative tribal areas, whereas KANU wanted a united country under a strong central government. KANU eventually won the pre-independence elections in May 1963, when Jomo Kenyatta became Prime Minister of Kenya. Britain gave formal independence to Kenya in December 1963, and on 12 December 1964 the Independent Republic of Kenya was born with Jomo Kenyatta as Kenya's first president. The distinctive black, red, green and white Kenya flag with a shield in the middle (black for black majority, red for the blood shed, green for land and white for the accepted, and welcome, white minority) now flew as the Union Jack was lowered in Nairobi for the very last time.

It was now decision time for the white Kenyans and their families. Many became jittery and resolved to sell up and leave Kenya, but my immediate family decided to stay, although George and his family left to live in England. Our family sold most of the land and property that my grandfather had fought so hard to achieve for ridiculously low prices. The farm in Kiambu was bought and quickly turned into a tourist hotel, whilst the coffee plants which had been tended for so many years with love sweat and tears were torn up and discarded.

The white families who remained in Kenya were happy to accept this new government and Jomo Kenyatta, or *Mzee* (Swahili for 'old man') as he was affectionately called, became a pragmatic and very popular president with all races. He coined the catchphrase *Harambee* (Swahili for 'let's all pull together'), encouraging white and black Kenyans to work together for the successful future of Kenya.

My parents continued to live in the house in Muthaiga (Number 44 Muthaiga Road) for many years, but sold it and their only other remaining property, the house on 'The Hill' in Nairobi, when they decided to leave Kenya and end their days living in England.

Miraculously the cycle continues with George Ernest's great granddaughter, our eldest daughter, her husband and three children who returned to live in Kenya and farm the land.

POSTCRIPT

RETURNING TO KENYA MANY YEARS LATER

Kenya today is a thriving, happy country with smart five-star hotels, luxury game lodges, tented camps and extensive flower farms. The house on 'The Hill' in Nairobi, where my parents lived when they were first married, and where I was born, has been demolished and replaced with a three storey office block, as has Gagee's little house next door. The house in Muthaiga, which my grandparents built and lived in until their deaths has also been razed and replaced with some expensive gated properties. Many of the original houses in this leafy suburb have become embassies, and property values are now Kenya's equivalent of London's Holland Park and Belgravia and there are many wealthy Kenyans who can afford to live in them.

Our spirits were raised when we visited what used to be the family farm, 'Kiltannon' in Kiambu, which is now a smart international hotel, the Windsor Country Hotel and Golf Club. We met the African owner, whose father had originally bought the farm from us, who was extremely charming and friendly. Contrary to what we had expected, although most of the land has been turned into a world-class golf course, he has kept some of the coffee, and was very interested to hear the history of the land and farm. We were pleased to see that all the original farm machinery and tractors (bought from Gailey & Roberts Ltd.) that my grandfather and uncle had used all those years ago are proudly on show. The house, which is set among trees away from the hotel, where George and his family once lived and where the new owners now reside, is unchanged.

GLOSSARY

Ayah	Nanny
Bibi	Woman, wife
Banda	Shed
Chai	Tea
Debbe	Empty kerosene container
Duka	Small shop
Fisi	Hyena
Gari	Motor vehicle
Hodi	Hello, can I come in, anyone at home?
Kanzu	Long white robe
Kiboko	Hippo, also a whip made of rhino hide
Lete chakula	Bring the food
Makuti	Thatch roof made from palm fronds
Memsahib	Mistress, lady
Mpishi	Cook
Mzee	Respectful term for 'old man'
Panga	Machete or large knife
Posho	Ground maize meal
Shamba	Small holding or garden
Siafu	Safari Ant
Simi	Short sword
Sufaria	Cooking pot
Shirka	Loin cloth dyed in yellow ochre
Safari	Journey
Tafadali	Please
Toto	Child
Topi	Hard bowl shaped hat made from the Indian solar plant

ACKNOWLEDGEMENTS

I cannot individually thank all the many kind friends who have read, re-read and checked passages for me, but a very special thanks must go to my lovely daughter-in-law, Emilie, for making the whole thing come together in her professional capacity.

To my great friend Robert for all his encouragement, input, advice and suggestions. To my friend Brenda for the many hours she spent scanning the photographs and typesetting my text. Heartfelt thanks to my wonderful friend, Jan, who painted the beautiful picture for the cover and to my late friend, David, for giving me his photograph of the lion from which the idea for the painting was taken. To my life-long friend, Judy, for letting me raid her photograph albums. Lastly, but certainly not least, to my cousin, Juliet, for sharing her memories, family papers and photographs with me.